Whitechapel & Spitalfields, East End London, 1888.

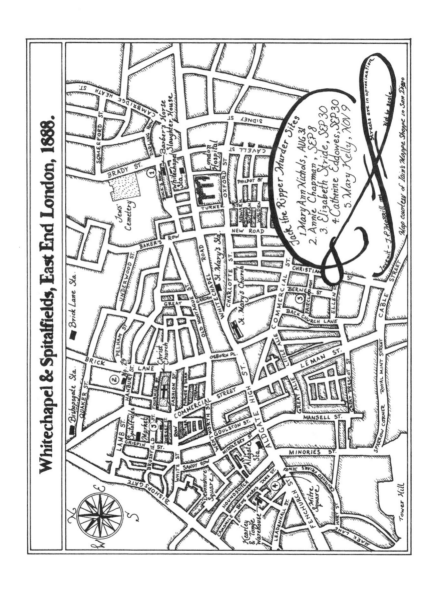

Jack the Ripper Murder Sites
1. Mary Ann Nichols, AUG 31
2. Annie Chapman, SEP 8
3. Elizabeth Stride, SEP 30
4. Catherine Eddowes, SEP 30
5. Mary Kelly, NOV 9

Streets are in approximation.
Not to scale.

Map courtesy of Jain's Wappe Shoppe in San Diego

JACK THE RIPPER
A Reference Guide

by
Scott Palmer

The Scarecrow Press, Inc.
Lanham, Md., & London

SCARECROW PRESS, INC.

Published in the United States of America
by Scarecrow Press, Inc.
4720 Boston Way, Lanham, Maryland 20706

4 Pleydell Gardens, Folkestone
Kent CT20 2DN, England

Copyright © 1995 by Scott Palmer

British Cataloging in Publication Information Available

Library of Congress Cataloging-in-Publication Data

Palmer, Scott, 1958–
Jack the Ripper : a reference guide / by Scott Palmer.
p.   cm.
Includes bibliographical references and index.
1. Jack, the Ripper.   2. Whitechapel (London, England)—
History.   I. Title.
HV6535.G6L6568   1995   364.1'523'09—dc20   95–1498

ISBN 0–8108–2996–7 (cloth : alk. paper)

Printed in the United States of America

 The paper used in this publication meets the minimum requirements of
American National Standard for Information Sciences—Permanence
of Paper for Printed Library Materials, ANSI Z39.48–1984.

CONTENTS

ACKNOWLEDGMENTS

I would like to thank the following organizations, institutions, and individuals for their assistance to me in the research of this book. Thanks to the Public Records Office (London), the *Times* of London, London Hospital, New Scotland Yard, Metropolitan Police (London), the *Daily Telegraph,* the *Evening Standard,* the *Criminologist,* the *Sun, Police Journal,* Guildhall Library, the British Museum, the *Lancet,* Guy's Hospital Archives, *Illustrated Police News, Daily Mail, Daily Express, East London Advertiser,* Chief Superintendent Anthony J. Forward (retired), author and former policeman Donald Rumbelow, and former policeman Martin Abel (retired). Also thanks to Joseph P. Morrill of Iain's Mappe Shoppe for providing the frontispiece map.

AUTHOR'S NOTE

For those readers seeking further or more detailed information on the individuals listed in this book, a consultation of your local library will prove most beneficial.

There have been some excellent biographies written on the more famous—such as Queen Victoria, Sir Charles Warren, Lord Salisbury, Lord Randolph Churchill, Prince Albert Victor, Coroner Wynne E. Baxter, etc. A fascinating book regarding recently alleged suspect James Maybrick was published by Smith Gryphon of London in 1993.

The best sources of information regarding the majority of those persons mentioned herewith in connection with the Ripper case—most of whom had somewhat minor significance–are the Home Office files and Scotland Yard files, which are housed at the Public Records Office at Kew, London, England. These files have been open to researchers of the case for nearly twenty years.

Newspaper morgues and files (such as those listed on the acknowledgments page) are invaluable sources for discovering contemporary accounts of the case, and also provide information on many of the lesser-known witnesses and suspects. The registrars of birth and death have yielded some hitherto unpublished information. Most of the books listed in the bibliography section provide useful information of one type or another.

INTRODUCTION

After more than a hundred years, the fascination with the identity of the Whitechapel murderer known as Jack the Ripper, who terrorized the East End of London in the summer and autumn of 1888, is growing rather than declining. There are many reasons for this, not the least of which is the vast number of books and articles, especially in the last decade, that have been written about the unknown killer.

There have been no end of theories and speculation regarding the Ripper's motives and identity, many of them quite farfetched. It is, however, a fact that (as far as we know) Jack the Ripper was never caught. At least no one was ever convicted of the crimes, or even brought to trial. Therein lies the fascination.

Numerous arrests were made at the time of the killings; a number of them were made to protect the suspect more than anything else, or to prevent possible riots.

This book is not a work of fiction; rather it is a compilation of fact, categorizing victims, suspects, police, politicians, doctors, coroners, witnesses, etc. Many of the recent books attempt to draw conclusions based on the character(s) their particular authors wish us to believe was Jack the Ripper, regardless of facts or evidence to support their claims. Some of them are fascinating, others simply ludicrous.

While this book is primarily concerned with listing the known facts of the case, there are few things one can discuss with absolute certainty, especially after the passage of more than a century.

It may at rare times be necessary, therefore, to speak in terms of probabilities, likelihoods, or unlikely circumstances. Very little can be ruled out as absolutely impossible, although some of the theories put forward by certain people require an extremely vivid imagination. The reader should keep an open mind and attempt to draw logical conclusions based on the known facts.

The suspects listed herewith are either those persons who were actually under suspicion or observation by the police in 1888, or who have come up in later works over the years. Unnamed suspects (such as "a butcher-slaughterman," "Jill the Ripper," "a mysterious doctor," etc.) are not included.

There has been much speculation as to the Ripper's anatomical or surgical skills (or the lack thereof). As one recent author of a Jack the Ripper book points out, there have been no authors heretofore on the subject of Jack the Ripper who have had medical training. I have in the past worked a number of years in a mortuary and am more than familiar with autopsies and the dissection of cadavers. I can therefore state with some degree of authority that Jack the Ripper most certainly had to have had some medical skills or training.

We can see clear evidence of this in the report of Dr. Frederick Gordon Brown on the body of Catherine Eddowes, the Mitre Square victim (s.v. "Brown" in Chapter 5 for full report). Eddowes's kidney had been carefully extracted, and any surgeon or coroner will verify (as does surgeon N. P. Warren in his 1989 article in the *Criminologist*) that the kidney is extremely difficult to expose from the front of the body, especially as it is hidden behind a membrane. Other organs were taken from victims carefully and wholly—when one remembers that these organs were removed in a very short time, most in almost total darkness, one can reasonably conclude the degree of skill necessary to do this would be even greater. Someone merely slashing about with a sharp instrument, with no knowledge or skill, inside a corpse would only make a mess. It would not be possible to remove these organs randomly or accidentally.

There have also been a number of theories having to do with Freemasonry and its involvement in these murders. While it is true that a great many of the high-ranking police and political figures in London in 1888 were Freemasons, apparently none of the authors of the books has himself been a Freemason, otherwise certain inaccuracies (and in some cases stupidities) would not have been written. As a Master Mason of good standing, I am worthy and well qualified to discuss this aspect (see Chapter 7, "Freemasonry").

We will probably never know beyond doubt the identity of Jack the Ripper, but with the passage of time the interest and fascination increases. This book is not designed to draw conclusions as to his identity; rather it is a work of reference endeavoring to list all of the principals involved, as well as some minor characters.

1. VICTIMS

Name	Date	Location of Body
Mary Ann Nichols	31 August 1888	Buck's Row
Annie Chapman	8 September 1888	29 Hanbury Street
Elizabeth Stride	30 September 1888	40 Berner Street
Catherine Eddowes	30 September 1888	Mitre Square
Mary Jane Kelly	9 November 1888	13 Miller's Court

The five victims above are those we can say with a great deal of certainty were slain by Jack the Ripper. Only Elizabeth Stride was not disemboweled; it is believed that the Ripper was frightened off by Louis Diemschutz's bringing his horse and cart into Dutfield's Yard—interrupted before he could finish his grisly work. All five of these women had their throats cut from left to right, suggesting a left-handed assailant.

Other women were murdered in the general vicinity before and after the abovementioned, but there is no conclusive evidence that they were Ripper victims, due to the dissimilarity of the methods of their murders; therefore, they will not be discussed.

MARY ANN NICHOLS (1845–1888)

The first victim of Jack the Ripper, Mary Ann Nichols, (or Nicholls), also known as "Polly," was born in 1845. Like the other Ripper victims, little is known of her early years. She was married to William Nichols, a printer, in 1864, and bore him five children.

After the breakup of her marriage in 1880 Nichols went to live with her father, Edward Walker, a locksmith and blacksmith living in Dean Street. She spent the next several years in and out of Lambeth Workhouse as well as with her father, whom she left in 1883 following a quarrel.

It was known as early as 1882 that Nichols had been earning her living by prostitution, at which time her husband cut off the weekly allowance he had been sending her.

In the summer of 1883, after yet another stay at Lambeth Workhouse, Nichols met one Thomas Drew, with whom she lived for the next four years in York Street, Walworth.

Subsequently she was back at Lambeth Workhouse, as well as other such institutions, on and off for the remainder of 1887 and until April 1888. At that time she obtained a position working for Mr. and Mrs. Samuel Cowdry at Ingleside, Wandsworth. This employment lasted for four months, until she absconded in mid-July, with some clothing valued at just over £3.

From that time until her death she stayed at doss houses in the East End, notably at 18 Thrawl Street and for the last week of her life at 56 Flower and Dean Street.

At half past midnight on Friday morning, 31 August, Nichols was seen at the Frying Pan public house in Brick Lane. About an hour later she was turned away from 18 Thrawl Street by the deputy because she did not have the necessary four shillings for a bed. She told the deputy to save her a bed as she would soon have the money and added, ''See what a jolly bonnet I've got now,'' as she left.

At 2:30 she met Emily Holland near Whitechapel High Street and told the latter that she had earned her doss money three times over but had drunk it away. Refusing to return with Holland to Thrawl Street, Polly Nichols went on her way and was never seen alive again (except by her killer).

Slightly more than an hour later, at about 3:40 A.M., a carman named Charles Cross (also referred to as George Cross), who was on his way to work, discovered the body in Buck's Row. He thought the body was a tarpaulin. A couple of minutes later another man, John (or Robert) Paul, a carter, also on his way to work, stopped. After looking at the body, which Paul thought was a drunk at first rather than a corpse, the two men fetched Police Constable Jonas Mizen from Hanbury Street (where the next murder was to take place) and directed him to the murdered woman.

Meanwhile, at 3:45 A.M. Police Constable John Neil was walking along his beat on Buck's Row when he came upon the body. Neil signaled to nearby patrolling Police Constable John Thain with his lamp; the latter came up and was soon joined by Mizen, who had been directed by Cross where to go.

Thain was sent to fetch a doctor directly. He returned with Dr. Rees Ralph Llewelyn, whom he had found at a surgery located at 152 Whitechapel Road. Three slaughtermen, employed at nearby Barber's Knacker's Yard, Winthrop Street, had returned with Neil to the murder site. They were Henry Tomkins, James Mumford, and Charles Brittain.

Dr. Llewelyn arrived in Buck's Row shortly after 4:00 A.M. and following a cursory examination pronounced Nichols to be dead. While the doctor was examining the corpse, Sergeant Kerby arrived. It was Kerby, with assistance from Thain, who later removed the body to the mortuary.

Thain remained at the murder site until Inspector John Spratling had been notified and arrived at 4:30. By this time the body had already been taken to the mortuary, and bloodstains in the street were being washed away by James Green, a resident of Buck's Row.

Spratling went to the mortuary to take down a description of the body, and there he discovered the full extent of the injuries when the body was stripped. Spratling sent for Dr. Llewelyn to make a further and more complete examination. Before he arrived, Robert Mann (or Munn) and James Hatfield washed the body, although the police had instructed them not to do so.

A laundry mark with the name of Lambeth Workhouse on a petticoat enabled the authorities to identify Mary Ann Nichols. She was formally identified at the mortuary by Mary Ann Monk of Lambeth Workhouse.

Although Nichols's husband, William, had not seen her for more than three years, he remarked upon viewing her body, "I forgive you for everything, now that I have seen you like this."

The *Star,* reporting on the murder related:

> No murder was ever more ferociously and brutally done. The knife, which must have been a large and sharp one, was jabbed into the deceased at the lower part of the abdomen and then drawn upwards not once but twice. The first cut veered to the

right, slitting up the groin and passing over the left hip, but the second cut went straight upward along the centre of the body, and reaching to the breast-bone. Such horrible work could only be the work of a maniac.

The inquest on the death of Mary Ann Nichols was held at the Working Lads' Institute in Whitechapel under the auspices of Coroner Wynne E. Baxter, opening on Saturday, 1 September, and reconvening on the third, seventeenth, and twenty-third.

Inspector John Spratling testified that he had been called to the murder scene and then went to the mortuary where he discovered the full extent of the mutilations. Spratling also stated that he, along with Sergeant George Godley, had searched the murder area, including the East London and District Railway embankments and Eastern Railway yard, but found no weapon and no bloodstains other than those that had been washed away.

Before the final outcome of the inquest, another sensational murder occurred.

ANNIE CHAPMAN (1841–1888)

The second Ripper victim, known as "Dark Annie" or "Annie Sivvey" (derived from her having lived with a sievemaker in 1886), was born in Paddington where she lived until she was fifteen, her father moving his family to Windsor in 1856.

She married coachman John Chapman in 1869 and bore him three children. Her marriage to him broke up in 1881, and he thereafter sent her an allowance until his death in 1886. Annie's alleged immoral behavior and drunkenness was the reason for the marital breakup.

Over the next couple of years, Annie sold flowers, matches, needlework, and herself. The last four months of her life she lived, for the most part, at Crossingham's, a common lodging house at 35 Dorset Street.

She received a black eye a day or days before her death in a fight with another prostitute, Eliza Cooper, regarding a florin and a piece of soap. Chapman told Amelia Palmer of the fight, also telling the latter that she would have to go out and get some money soon or she would lose her lodgings.

Just after midnight on 8 September, the day of her murder, Annie Chapman was seen in the kitchen at Crossingham's by the deputy, Timothy Donovan, and William Stevens. The two men noticed that she was in a slightly inebriated condition. A few minutes later she went out for a drink but was back once again at 1:30 A.M., at which time Donovan asked her for her doss money. She told Donovan that she had been ill and in the infirmary and did not have it, but added on her way out, "Don't let my bed; I'll be back soon." She also told watchman John Evans to make sure that Donovan kept a bed for her.

From that time onward she apparently plied her trade; Elizabeth Darrell later reported seeing a woman (who she subsequently identified as Chapman in the mortuary) and man talking on the pavement at 29 Hanbury Street at about 5:30 A.M.

Albert Cadoche, a carpenter residing at 27 Hanbury Street, reported hearing some noises emanating from the backyard of the building next door at about the same time, when he left for work. He noticed no one outside his residence in the street.

John Davis, an elderly carman who lived at 29 Hanbury Street, went into the backyard at 5:45 A.M. and discovered the mutilated body of Annie Chapman. The horrified Davis went down to Barclay's packing case shop at 23a Hanbury Street and excitedly told James Green and James Kent of his grisly discovery. Green and Kent went to have a look at the corpse and then to Commercial Street Police Station. It was from this station that Inspector Joseph Chandler, the senior duty officer, went to Hanbury Street at 6:00 A.M.

Upon arriving, Chandler ordered the clearing out of a small crowd that had already begun to gather at the scene. He also ordered the body to be covered with sacking.

H Division Police Surgeon Dr. George Bagster Phillips was sent for and arrived at Hanbury Street at about 6:30. It did not take Phillips but an instant to officially and formally certify that Chapman was dead. Her throat had been cut down to the backbone, the body had been disemboweled, and part of the intestine had been unceremoniously draped over the left shoulder (s.v. "Phillips" in Chapter 5 for further details).

Phillips noted the contents of the victim's pockets and other items lying nearby on the ground, while Chandler searched the yard for any clues. One thing that was remarked upon at the time was a leather apron saturated with water, which was later identified as belonging to John Richardson, a resident of 29 Hanbury Street.

Dr. Phillips gave instructions that the body be removed to the mortuary, and he arrived there himself at 2:00 that afternoon to conduct a full postmortem. He was annoyed to discover that the body, like that of Mary Ann Nichols, had been stripped of its clothing and washed.

Amelia Palmer had made the formal identification of the body of Annie Chapman at 11:30 on the morning of her murder. Once again, Coroner Wynne E. Baxter presided over the inquest, which was held at the Working Lads' Institute in Whitechapel Road on 10 September 1888.

Due to the extreme heat, the graphic nature and details of the case, and overcrowding, several spectators passed out. It was at that point that Baxter decided to clear the court for Dr. Phillips's testimony. Phillips stated that in his opinion it would have taken an expert no less than fifteen minutes to produce the multilations.

The doctor's findings were so horrific that the *Times* of London did not see fit to publish them. In the *Lancet,* however, appeared the following:

> The abdomen had been entirely laid open; the intestines, severed from their mesenteric attachments, had been lifted out of her body and placed on the shoulder of the corpse; whilst from the pelvis, the uterus and its appendages, with the upper portion of the vagina and the posterior two-thirds of the bladder, had been entirely removed. No trace of these parts could be found.

Following the Chapman murder, the East End of London was stirred to a frenzy. Police made numerous arrests, a good many to protect the suspects from mob violence. Most arrested were released almost immediately. Some were not so lucky; they were sent to an asylum.

On 10 September, the same day as the inquest on Annie Chapman, two notable events occurred. The first was the arrest of John Pizer, a boot-finisher, by Sergeant William Thicke in the morning hours at 22 Mulberry Street. I have already mentioned the discovery of the Richardson leather apron in the backyard at 29 Hanbury Street. This leather apron was widely publicized and created a public distrust toward any person known to wear such an item regularly.

Pizer wore a leather apron in his vocation, and his description matched that of a suspect who was described in the press as "an unknown local Jew who has been ill-using prostitutes in the East End."

Pizer had been in the vicinity of the London Dock Fire when Nichols was killed, talking to a policeman at 1:30 A.M. Pizer denied that he had been in Hanbury Street on 7/8 September, and because of lack of evidence, was released after about a thirty-six hour incarceration.

Subsequently, Pizer filed and won several lawsuits against newspapers who had described him variously as "half man, half beast," "a cunning Jew," "a monster, ghoulish," etc.

The second noteworthy event of the day occurred in the evening. This was the formation of the Whitechapel Vigilance Committee, made up of sixteen ratepayers, and headed by builder George Lusk. The meeting was held at the Crown public house, Mile End Road. Members of the committee made themselves available to the public in order to receive suggestions, and even wrote to Scotland Yard offering their assistance and suggesting a reward be offered to help identify the killer.

ELIZABETH STRIDE (1843–1888)

Jack the Ripper's third victim was a native of Gothenburg, Sweden, who emigrated to London in 1866. She married a ship's carpenter and later coffeehouse proprietor John T. Stride in 1869. The couple had nine children before their marriage broke up in 1882.

John Stride died in 1884, and the following year "Long Liz," as Elizabeth Stride was also known, moved in with a laborer named Michael Kidney, with whom she lived on and off for the remaining three years of her life.

During 1887 and 1888 she was arrested quite a number of times for drunkenness, disorderly conduct and other related misdemeanors. She was convicted of these charges no fewer than eight times.

Dr. Barnardo, famous founder of boys' homes, observed Stride on a visit to lodgings at No. 32 Flower and Dean Street, where the latter apparently lived during the month of September 1888.

She was seen in the general vicinity of the lodging house by many people several hours before her death. Witnesses saw her in the Bricklayer's Arms public house at 11:00 P.M. on 29 September. About forty-five minutes later she was observed in Berner Street near the place where her body was discovered, and somewhere about midnight grocer Matthew Packer sold a bunch of black grapes to a man who was with her.

In fact, Stride apparently did not stray far away from the place where she was killed for the last hour or so of her life. She was seen by both Packer and Police Constable William Smith near the entrance gate of Dutfield's Yard at 12:30 A.M., 30 September. About a quarter of an hour later she was observed by James Brown at the end of the street, and Israel Schwartz saw her thrown to the pavement by a man at about ten minutes to one, but Schwartz continued on his way.

Jewelry salesman Louis Diemschutz was returning to the International Workingmen's Educational Club, to which he was steward, at 1:00 A.M. The club was frequented primarily by Jewish socialists, intellectuals, and radicals. The club bordered the north side of Dutfield's Yard, and it was into this yard that Diemschutz occasionally drove and parked his cart.

A light rain was falling as Diemschutz's pony pulled the cart through the wide-open gates of Dutfield's Yard. Just as the animal entered into the yard through the gates, it shied to the left and would go no farther. Diemschutz tried to get the pony to continue, but soon realized that something was frightening it or was in its way. Prodding about in the darkness with his whip, Diemschutz felt an object slightly yielding. Alighting from the cart, he struck a match and discovered the body of Elizabeth Stride, whom he at first thought to be drunk or unconscious.

He then went into the club, where he found Morris Eagle and Isaac Kozebrodsky, two club members who returned with him to the body, where they discovered that Stride's throat had been cut and she was dead. They also noticed that the body was quite warm.

Diemschutz, who afterward reckoned that the Ripper may have been just a few feet away from him and invisible in the inky blackness of the yard when he first entered, went off with a man called Jacobs in search of a policeman and met horse keeper Edward Spooner. The three men returned to the yard and observed the body for a few minutes before the police arrived.

Meanwhile, Morris Eagle had found police constables Edward Collins and Henry Lamb patrolling nearby and brought them back to the scene of the murder, where a small group comprised of club members and a few passersby and residents had already gathered. Collins then left to fetch a doctor.

Dr. William Blackwell arrived at a quarter past one and stated positively that Stride had been dead for no more than twenty minutes. Dr. Phillips was also sent for and arrived at Dutfield's Yard at 2:00 A.M. By this time another horrible murder had taken place not far away.

The inquest on Elizabeth Stride was conducted once more by Coroner Wynne E. Baxter, beginning the following day, 1 October, and is particularly notable for the absence of certain witnesses and facts that did not get into the record.

Despite the fact that police had taken their statements, neither Matthew Packer nor Israel Schwartz were called to testify at the inquest. Both men saw Stride with a man (not necessarily the same one) from a quarter of an hour to a half an hour before she was murdered, and it seems a gross stupidity (rather than the cover-up that some authors have suggested) that they were not called to give evidence.

The omission of Packer especially seems absurd. It was two private detectives who first elicited from him that he had sold half a pound of black grapes to a man accompanying Stride. He later identified her body at the mortuary; the detectives had shown him another body first to test his reliability. There are conflicting reports of a stem or stalk of grapes seen near the body, but it is a fact that Grand and Batchelor, the private detectives, recovered a grape stalk from a gutter a few yards from the murder scene.

Some authors have made the error of writing that Packer's evidence conflicts with that of Dr. Phillips, who conducted the postmortem and testified that Stride's stomach contents did not include any grapes, leading Phillips to conclude that Stride had not eaten any for several hours before her death. These authors have used flawed reasoning, and would do well to read Packer's official statement to the police, which the fruiterer gave personally to Sir Charles Warren on the afternoon of 4 October. Packer states that he sold the grapes to the man, not Stride, and although he had the couple under observation for half an hour, he never stated either to the police or to the press that he saw Stride eat any of the grapes. Since Phillips's analysis found no grapes, it is logical to assume that she ate none.

Coroner Baxter conducted the Stride inquiry without flamboyance or any of the dramatics or histrionics of the previous inquests.

The evidence of Constable Smith and James Brown led to the following description of the suspect published in the *Police Gazette:*

> At 12:35 a.m. on 30th September, with Elizabeth Stride found murdered the same date in Berner Street at 1:00 a.m., a man, age 28, height 5 feet 8 inches, complexion dark, small moustache; dress, black diagonal coat, hard felt hat, collar and tie, respectable appearance, carried a parcel wrapped up in newspaper.
>
> At 12:45 a.m., 30th, with the same woman in Berner Street, a man, age about 30, height 5 feet 5 inches; complexion fair, hair dark, small brown moustache, full face, broad shoulders; dress, dark jacket and trousers, black cap with peak.

CATHERINE EDDOWES (1842–1888)

As a child, Catherine Eddowes, born in Wolverhampton, attended St. John's Charity School in Bermondsey until her mother died when Catherine was thirteen. From that time on she and her brothers and sisters went to the Bermondsey Workhouse and Industrial School.

Afterward she was educated at Dowgate Charity School, Wolverhampton, while living with her aunt in nearby Biston Street. Around 1862 she met former soldier Thomas Conway, whom she claimed to have married, although no record of the marriage has been found. The couple had two sons and a daughter.

Eddowes and Conway parted company in 1880 and the following year she met market porter John Kelly, with whom she lived for the remaining seven years of her life.

During the month of September 1888, Eddowes and Kelly went hop picking in Kent. They did not have much luck, however, and returned to London on 28 September. The couple took rooms in separate lodging houses, although they apparently still maintained their residence in Flower and Dean Street.

Eddowes told the deputy of her lodging house that she knew the identity of Jack the Ripper, and was out to claim the reward. Although many people made such claims during the Ripper scare, Eddowes may have been doing more than simply mouthing off, as two days later she was to become the fourth victim.

The following morning she was reunited with Kelly, and pawned a pair of his boots. By early afternoon, however, the couple was without funds once again, having bought a meal and a number of drinks. Eddowes decided that she could get some money from her daughter, who was now married and living in Southwark, so off she went. Whether her daughter gave her any money cannot be verified. It is reasonable to assume that she got some money somewhere, as she was next seen back in the East End by evening and was apparently quite drunk.

At 8:30 P.M. she was observed in Aldgate Street lying on the pavement making noises like a fire engine. She was arrested for creating a disturbance by Police Constable Louis Robinson, who with the assistance of another constable, George Simmons, took her to Bishopsgate Police Station, where she was formally charged and put in a cell. It was customary procedure at the time for persons to be kept in the cells until they had become reasonably sober and then released in their own custody. At 12:30 A.M., 30 September, Eddowes seemed to be in a much better condition than when she was brought in. She asked if she could be released.

Police Constable George Hutt, who had come on duty at 9:45, or about three hours beforehand, evidently felt that Eddowes was now in control of herself, so he released her from custody at about one o'clock. After some light banter between the two, Hutt watched her go off, heading in the direction of Mitre Square. At the same time, not far away in Dutfield's Yard, Berner Street, Louis Diemschutz was just making the discovery of the corpse of Elizabeth Stride.

At about half past one a woman later identified as Eddowes from her clothing was seen standing with a man at the entryway to Mitre Square.

Three men—Joseph Lawende, Harry Harris, and Joseph Levy—who had remained late at the nearby Imperial Club on account of the rain, noticed the couple, but only Lawende got a good look at the man, whose appearance suggested nothing unusual or exciting to him.

A policeman, Constable James Harvey, was passing on his beat at the exact spot where the couple had been seen by the three men less than ten minutes later, or at 1:40 A.M. He reported afterward seeing or hearing nothing suspicious.

Although Harvey did not actually enter the square, another policeman did five minutes later, at about 1:45 A.M. His name was Edward Watkins, and his beat intersected that of Harvey's, Watkins approaching Mitre Square from the opposite direction.

He discovered the body in the southwest corner of the square, and immediately went to a nearby warehouse, owned by Kearley and Tonge where he called night watchman and former policeman George Morris, who was known to him.

"For God's sake, mate, come to assist me . . . here's another woman cut up to pieces," shouted Watkins. Morris returned with Watkins to the square, took a look at the body, and then ran off blowing his whistle, which was answered by Harvey, who was not far away. Police Constable Holland also arrived and went immediately to fetch Dr. George Sequeira from 34 Jewry Street.

Sequeira arrived at 1:45 A.M. to pronounce Eddowes officially dead; he awaited the arrival of Dr. Frederick Gordon Brown, the City of London police surgeon, as Mitre Square lies in the square mile that comes under the jurisdiction of the City Police. Brown arrived a little over a quarter of an hour later to make a more detailed examination (for his report, s.v. "Brown" in Chapter 5).

Detective Alfred Foster and Superintendent James McWilliam of the City Police were the next to arrive at the scene, followed by City Police Commissioner Sir Henry Smith. Certain items found near the body as well as her clothing helped to identify Catherine Eddowes.

The body was removed to Golden Lane Mortuary at about the same time that Police Constable Alfred Long discovered a piece of Eddowes's apron and a chalked message on the wall in Goulston Street. The apron helped to determine the direction in which the Ripper went after he killed Eddowes. There was further evidence that he washed blood off his hands in a nearby public sink.

The inquest opened on 4 October and reconvened on the eleventh of the month under the direction of Coroner Samuel Langham, who conducted it forthrightly and without the pomp and ceremony of the early Baxter inquests.

John Kelly formally identified the body of Eddowes but denied knowledge of the fact that she was a prostitute, which doubtless was in his own self-interest, as he could have been charged with living off immoral earnings. Other witnesses at the inquest described Catherine Eddowes as a cheerful and good-natured person.

Dr. Brown gave his evidence, which in detail described the condition of the body and also included his findings in reference to the knife used for the horrible dissection. As with three other Ripper victims, the uterus was missing, as was the left kidney, which required definite anatomical knowledge and skill. The ears had also been nicked or clipped.

Two points in Brown's testimony are especially memorable and were a portent of things shortly to come. The first point was about the condition of the ears. Police received a letter signed "Jack the Ripper," giving him the name which was to become legendary. The letter mentioned "a double event," and continued on to say that the killer would "clip the lady's ears off and send them to the police officers just for jolly."

This letter, known as the "Dear Boss" letter because of its form of address, was mostly likely from the killer because it was sent to Scotland Yard on the day before the two murders—i.e., 29 September 1888.

The second notable point was regarding the kidney of Catherine Eddowes, which had been removed by the killer. As previously mentioned, this organ cannot be randomly or accidentally removed wholly and carefully as it was in this case. It is located behind a membrane, and unless one is familiar with its whereabouts, one would not know where to find it. Two things were needed by the killer: knowledge and skill—knowledge to know where it was, and skill to remove it.

George Lusk, president of the Whitechapel Vigilance Committee, received a small cardboard box through the post on 16 October, accompanied by a letter, most probably from the Ripper (see Chapter 8, "Poems and Letters"). Besides the letter was enclosed a human kidney. Lusk thought that it was a rather sick joke, believing the organ to be an animal's. The letter, which was addressed "From Hell," went on to say, in part, that the killer had fried and eaten a portion of the kidney, and if Lusk would be patient, the killer just might send him his knife.

It is almost certain that this kidney was the missing Eddowes organ. Lusk took the kidney to Dr. Thomas Openshaw, consulting surgeon at London Hospital. Sir Henry Smith later stated that the kidney had also been examined by Dr. Henry Sutton, senior surgeon at the same institution. Both men agreed that it was a human kidney that had been removed about two weeks previously and preserved in spirits of wine. This proves beyond doubt that the kidney came from no hospital, mortuary, or other institution, as formaldehyde is and was in 1888 used in these cases. It was also noted that the kidney contained Bright's disease, which was evident in the kidney remaining in Eddowes's body according to the report of Dr. Brown. Finally, the length of renal artery attached to the kidney corresponded *exactly* to the piece remaining in the body. These facts prove beyond speculation that the kidney received by Lusk was that of Catherine Eddowes; there are too many coincidences to draw any other logical conclusion.

MARY JANE KELLY (1863–1888)

There is not a great deal of information available on the early life of Jack the Ripper's final victim because searches of the records have provided few facts.

By her own account, Mary Kelly was a native of Limerick, Ireland, who moved with her family to Wales, where her father worked as an ironmonger. She supposedly married a collier named Davis, or Davies, about 1879 and turned to prostitution when her husband was killed in a mining explosion.

It has also been suggested by researchers and storytellers that Kelly was the linchpin in a conspiracy to blackmail the royal family and government, which led to the murders.

Mary Kelly was supposedly a West End prostitute who went to Paris for a short time in the company of a man, possibly the artist Walter Sickert. Later she allegedly worked in a shop in Cleveland Street where Prince Albert Victor, grandson of Queen Victoria, supposedly met and "married" one Annie Crook, siring an illegitimate daughter to whom Kelly acted as nursemaid.

Most of what we know for sure about Mary Kelly begins in 1887, when she met fish-market porter Joseph Barnett, with whom she lived at various addresses in Spitalfields and White-chapel until her death in November 1888. Their final address was number 13 Miller's Court, where Mary was found murdered. After an argument on 30 October, Barnett left Miller's Court to take up lodgings elsewhere, although he still came around to see Kelly. This argument was reported to stem from the fact that Kelly allowed several other prostitutes to stay in her room.

On Thursday, 8 November, Kelly was seen in and around Miller's Court all day. She spent the afternoon in the company of another prostitute, Maria Harvey, and Barnett visited her later in the evening, from 7:30 until about 8:00. After Barnett left, Kelly began drinking and plying her trade, as she was observed in several public houses and around the court talking to prospective clients beginning at approximately 11:00 P.M. Mary Ann Cox saw Kelly in the entrance to Miller's Court with a client about fifteen minutes before midnight, and a number of people, mostly residents of the court, heard her singing on and off for the next hour.

At 2:00 A.M. Friday, 9 November, George Hutchinson, a recently unemployed resident of nearby Commercial Street and an acquaintance of Kelly, had a short conversation with her near Flower & Dean Street. Kelly asked Hutchinson for sixpence, to which he replied that he had spent all his money. Kelly then said to him, "Good morning, I must go and find some money."

Hutchinson next observed a man approaching Kelly from the opposite direction, and he followed the pair back to the entrance of Miller's Court. Hutchinson made a mental note of the man, who struck him as suspicious and gave him a dirty look. Hutchinson waited outside the court for about three-quarters of an hour, then went home.

Although Hutchinson clearly got a good look at the man and gave the police a detailed description of him, he was not called as a witness at Kelly's inquest. Hutchinson also thought he recognized the man a couple days after the murder.

Other residents of or visitors to the court either saw or heard Kelly during the next hour. At approximately 4:00 A.M. Elizabeth Prater, who lived in the room directly above Kelly, was awakened by her kitten, Diddles, and heard a cry of "Murder" emanating from somewhere nearby. Since cries of this sort were not uncommon in the area, Prater paid no further attention and went back to sleep. Nothing more was seen or heard of Kelly for almost seven hours, when she was found butchered.

At 10:45 A.M. Thomas Bowyer went to No. 13 to collect from Kelly the back rent that she owed landlord John McCarthy. Receiving no reply to his knocks on the door (which was, incidentally, locked), Bowyer was able to pull back the curtain by means of a broken window and saw the horrifying sight inside. He ran to fetch McCarthy, who took one look through the window at the carnage and ran to Commercial Road Police Station, where he found Inspector Walter Beck. Beck returned to Miller's Court with McCarthy, and with Sergeants George Godley and Edward Badham, as well as Walter Dew. Inspector Frederick Abberline arrived at 11:30 A.M.

Soon after it became common knowledge that another horrific murder had been committed, a crowd began gathering, some of the people anticipating the Lord Mayor's Parade, which was to pass by shortly.

Because of Sir Charles Warren's experiments with the champion bloodhounds Burgho and Barnaby (see Chapter 4 "Politicians and Police," "Sir Charles Warren" entry for further discussion), the room was not entered until 1:30 P.M., by which time Warren had resigned and the dogs were no longer available. The door to Kelly's room, which was spring locked, was smashed in by McCarthy with an axe handle. Superintendent Thomas Arnold had recently arrived, and it was on his orders that McCarthy broke down the door.

Drs. Thomas Bond and George Bagster Phillips were in attendance and made their examination of the most grossly mutilated victim of Jack the Ripper before the body was removed to Shoreditch Mortuary later that afternoon. The postmortem was conducted by Phillips, Bond, and Frederick Gordon Brown.

The inquest, which began on 12 November, was held under the eye of Roderick MacDonald at Shoreditch Town Hall. Jurors were confused by the fact that MacDonald was heading the inquiry, as Kelly was murdered in an area that came under the jurisdiction of Coroner Wynne Baxter, who had held inquests on three previous victims. MacDonald snapped back at a juror that the body was now lying in a place that came under his jurisdiction—never mind where the murder took place.

MacDonald has been criticized for the way he handled the inquest, and this criticism seems justified. This was the only inquest on a Ripper victim to be concluded the same day it began, and considering the fact that Kelly was the last victim, the only one killed indoors, and the most horribly mutilated, this seems incredible.

MacDonald seems to have had a poor attitude and to have acted both obstinately and stupidly. His failure to ask relevant questions and call important witnesses (especially George Hutchinson) is unbelievable.

2. WITNESSES

The following persons were witnesses who gave evidence to the press, police, or at an inquest, as to seeing the victims with or without various suspects. Some of these witnesses knew or saw the victims, either alive or dead.

There are many "witnesses" to one thing or another, but for the purpose of this reference I will list only those who had a direct bearing on the case. Persons who, for example, saw someone with blood on his clothing or acting suspiciously at irrelevant times will not be included. By the same token, neither will those who merely knew a victim, unless they saw or spoke to her at a significant time, or gave evidence at the inquest.

For convenience, I have listed witnesses separately under the name of the victim they knew or saw, generally in the order of their importance. Police and doctors are listed elsewhere.

THE CASE OF MARY ANN NICHOLS

William Nichols

William Nichols was the husband of Mary Ann Nichols and the father of their five children, who were born between 1866 and 1879. A printer by trade, he married Mary Ann, née Walker, in 1864.

Their marriage broke up in 1880 after Mary had been known to be habitually drunk and ran away from home at least half a dozen times, although *her* family claimed that the breakup was due in part to some infidelity by William.

Nichols paid his wife a weekly allowance until 1882, at which time he learned that his wife was earning her living as a prostitute. She tried to get the courts to have Nichols restore this maintenance, but on evidence of her conduct they ruled in his favor.

Nichols did not see Mary Ann alive after 1885. Upon viewing her body at the mortuary, Nichols said, ''I forgive you for everything, now that I have seen you like this.''

Emily Holland

The last person known to have seen Mary Ann Nichols alive, Holland met her at approximately 2:30 A.M. on 31 August 1888 near Whitechapel High Street.

After Nichols told her that she had earned her doss money thrice over but had drank it away, Holland tried to get Nichols to accompany her back to 18 Thrawl Street, where they both lodged, but Nichols refused.

Holland went to the mortuary where she identified ''Polly'' Nichols, and later gave evidence at the inquest. Some authors believe Emily Holland to be the same as Jane Oram, who also gave evidence, but the great dissimilarity between the two names makes this seem unlikely.

Charles Cross

A carman who worked in Broad Street and was sometimes referred to as George Cross, he was on his way to work in Buck's Row at 3:45 A.M. when he came upon Nichols's body, which he at first mistook for an abandoned tarpaulin. He was joined a very few minutes later by John Paul, also on his way to work, and after an examination of the body determined Nichols was dead. Cross next went with Paul to Hanbury Street where they found Police Constable Jonas Mizen and directed him to the body. Cross also gave evidence at the inquest.

John Paul

A carter employed in nearby Hanbury Street and sometimes referred to as Robert Paul, he was walking down Buck's Row on his way to work when he came upon Charles Cross, who had just discovered Nichols. Paul believed at first that the woman was drunk but it was soon easily determined that she was in fact dead. Paul, who later testified to all that happened, said that he and Cross went to Hanbury Street where, after telling P.C. Mizen what they had found, he continued on to work.

Henry Tomkins

Described by the newspapers as "a tough-looking bloke," Henry Tomkins was a slaughterman who lived in Bethnal Green and worked in nearby Barber's Knacker's Yard. Tomkins, along with fellow slaughtermen Charles Brittain and James Mumford, was told about the murder, possible by a policeman. He was at the site at 4:00 A.M. when P.C. Thain returned with Dr. Llewelyn. Tomkins gave evidence at the inquest regarding the position of the body as he had seen it.

James Mumford

Like Henry Tomkins, a slaughterman at Barber's Knacker's Yard, Winthrop Street, he saw Nichols's body just after four o'clock in the morning. He said in a statement to the press that P.C. Thain had informed him of the murder, but Thain denied this, saying that he first noticed Mumford and two other men when he returned with Dr. Llewelyn.

Mumford remained at the murder site with Thain until Sergeant Kerby removed the body to the mortuary.

Charles Brittain

Employed at Barber's Knacker's Yard as well, Brittain arrived in Buck's Row with his two coworkers. It is not known for certain whether the three men were on their way to work or were already there when they heard about the crime. Brittain apparently went back to work after seeing the body, Mumford remaining at the scene.

Mary Ann Monk

Following the discovery of a Lambeth Workhouse label or laundry mark on one of the petticoats that had been worn by Nichols, Mary Ann Monk of Lambeth Workhouse went to the mortuary and formally identified the body. She also gave evidence at the inquest.

James Hatfield

An elderly pauper living in Whitechapel Workhouse, Hatfield, with Robert Mann, stripped and later washed the body of Nichols, even though Detective Sergeant Enright told him not to. Hatfield was admonished by a juror for his poor memory, but Coroner Baxter went easy with the old fellow.

Robert Mann (*or* Munn)

At the Nichols inquest, Coroner Baxter instructed the jury to disregard the evidence of this epileptic mortuary attendant who assisted Hatfield with the body. Mann's answers to questions about whether the police gave instructions to lay out the body or not to touch it show confusion.

Harriet Lilley

A resident of Buck's Row, living two doors away from where the body lay, Mrs. Lilley testified that she was awakened by gasps and moans followed by whispers about 3:30 A.M. She woke her husband; they both continued to listen for a time, but hearing nothing further, went back to sleep.

Sarah Colwell

Living at the end of Buck's Row, Mrs. Colwell claimed she heard a woman running and shouting in the wee hours of the morning of

31 August. Police disregarded her claim that she saw blood in the
street the following day. She was not called as a witness.

Thomas Ede

An inquest witness, Ede testified that he had seen a man outside
a public house near the time of the killing with a sharp knife
sticking out of his pocket. The man was later identified as Henry
James, a harmless local lunatic.

Emma Green

Another resident of Buck's Row, in fact living just a few feet from
where the body was found, she testified she neither saw nor heard
anything unusual. James Green, her son (not to be confused with
James Green, the Chapman witness) washed away the blood in the
street after Nichols was taken away.

Patrick Mulshaw

A night porter in Winthrop Street, Mulshaw testified that an
unknown man passed him in the street about 4:00 A.M. and said,
"Watchman, old man, I believe somebody is murdered down the
street." He went to look at the body, recognizing Henry Tomkins
as one of the men already there.

Jane Oram

A witness who gave evidence at the Nichols inquest, she said she
saw Nichols in or near the Frying Pan in Brick Lane. She is
sometimes confused with Emily Holland because of similar
evidence; the two names are nothing alike.

Walter Purkiss

The manager of Essex Wharf, directly across from Buck's Row,
Purkiss testified that neither he nor his wife heard or saw anything

unusual on the night of the murder, even though it was very quiet and they both woke periodically throughout the night.

THE CASE OF ANNIE CHAPMAN

John Davis

An elderly carman who lived with his wife and three sons at 29 Hanbury Street, Davis was employed in Leadenhall Market.

Davis, after tossing and turning for some time, got up and prepared to go to work. By 5:45 A.M., 8 September 1888, he was ready, and upon going out through the backyard he discovered the horribly mutilated remains of Annie Chapman.

Davis excitedly raced off a few doors down the street to Bayley's Packing Case Shop at No. 23a Hanbury Street, and there found James Kent and James Green. The two men returned with Davis to the yard and found the body. While the others went to have a drink, Davis ran to nearby Commercial Street Police Station, where Inspector Joseph Chandler was told of the crime. Chandler arrived at the scene at six o'clock. Davis told all this to Baxter at the inquest, which began on 10 September.

Timothy Donovan

The deputy of Crossingham's Lodging House, Donovan, along with William Stevens, noticed an intoxicated Annie Chapman in the lodging house kitchen after midnight.

After Chapman went out and returned once again, Donovan asked her for her doss money, which she did not have. This was about 1:45 A.M.

Donovan testified to this at the inquest, also remembering that Chapman asked him at the same time to save her a bed as she was planning to return. He also told the police that he knew a man known as "Leather Apron," having recently ejected him from the lodging house.

Amelia Palmer

Charwoman for East End residents following an accident to her husband, dock laborer Henry Palmer, Amelia was a friend of Annie Chapman and formally identified her body at 11:30 A.M. on the day of the murder.

Chapman told Palmer of a fight she had had with Eliza Cooper a day or days before and also stated that she would have to get some money soon or lose her lodgings.

Mrs. Palmer gave Chapman twopence several days before she died, suggesting Chapman spend it on food and not drink, as Chapman had been feeling unwell, possibly as the result of the aforementioned fight. At the inquest, Amelia Palmer furnished some biographical data on Chapman, which she had also provided to the police.

Eliza Cooper

A prostitute and acquaintance of the deceased who also resided at the time at Crossingham's Lodging House, Cooper testified at the inquest that she had had a fight with Chapman the week of her death and gave the latter a black eye, but was reticent about giving details of the reason for the fight. Others claimed the fight started when Cooper stole a piece of soap from Chapman and a florin from a local character known as Harry the Hawker.

Cooper also told the press that she had information as to the whereabouts of "Leather Apron," who she said lived in the district.

Albert Cadoche (b. 1857)

A carpenter residing at 27 Hanbury Street, Cadoche testified that he heard a woman say "No!" at about 5:30 on the morning of the murder. He thought the sound came from the next backyard. He then heard a sound like something or someone falling against the fence that separated Nos. 27 and 29.

Cadoche left for work at 5:32, and noticed no one around the front of his own residence or the building next door.

Henry Holland

A resident of Aden Road, Mile End, Holland was on his way to work when he was informed of the finding of the body by the excited Davis.

After looking at the corpse, Holland went to Spitalfields Market, where he found a policeman who refused to accompany Holland back to the scene. Later that afternoon Holland went to Commercial Street Police Station where he made a formal complaint against the policeman regarding his conduct.

James Green

A workman at Bayley's Packing Case Shop, located at 23a Hanbury Street, Green was on the premises when John Davis ran up shouting that there had been a murder a few yards away. In the company of his coworker James Kent, Green accompanied Davis to the backyard of No. 29, where he saw the body of Annie Chapman.

Green, who gave his evidence at the Chapman inquest, is not to be confused with the younger James Green, who washed away the bloodstains in the street in Buck's Row after the Nichols murder.

James Kent

Like the aforementioned, a worker at Bayley's Packing Case Shop, he was told about the murder by the excited carman Davis.

Kent testified at the inquest; he also gave an interview to the *East London Observer* a few days later. Their correspondent found Kent an interesting witness. Kent said that after viewing the body he had to have a stiff drink, and later fetched a canvas to cover the body on orders from Inspector Chandler.

William Stevens

He testified that his occupation was printer, and his residence was Crossingham's Lodging House, where the deceased also lodged.

Along with deputy Donovan, Stevens noticed Chapman in the kitchen just after midnight, eating a baked potato and afterward putting some pills in an envelope that she had taken from the mantelpiece. Stevens also believed Chapman to be somewhat intoxicated.

John Evans

The night watchman at Crossingham's, elderly John Evans (known affectionately as "Brummy") last saw Chapman about 1:30 A.M. on the day of her death.

Evans noted the drunken appearance of Chapman and remembered that on her way out the door she reminded him to be sure to tell Donovan to save a bed for her, as she intended to return shortly.

Elizabeth Long

Also variously described as Elizabeth Darrell, or Durrell, Long identified Chapman's body at the mortuary on 12 September.

She told the police and the press that on the morning of the eighth of that month at about 5:30, she had seen a man and woman engaged in conversation near the entrance to the yard gate at 29 Hanbury Street, and when she went to the mortuary she identified Chapman as the same woman.

Sarah Cox

Sara Cox was an elderly woman residing upstairs at 29 Hanbury Street, living on a small income and cared for in part by Mrs. Richardson.

When interviewed about the murder, she stated that she had been asleep and neither saw nor heard anything at all from her third-floor room, which overlooked the backyard.

John Richardson

A packing case worker at Spitalfields Market, his mother lived at 29 Hanbury Street. Richardson went there at 4:45 A.M. on the day of the murder to fix a lock. At one point he sat down to cut a piece of leather off one of his boots. He testified to this, and was asked to produce his knife. It was ascertained that the knife could not have been used by the murderer.

It was Richardson's leather apron that was seen in the backyard next to a tap, saturated with water. Its discovery was widely publicized and helped to create the sensation of the ''Leather Apron'' scare.

Richardson went on to testify that he had remained in the yard only a few minutes and saw or heard nothing unusual. The first he knew about the murder was when he heard someone discussing it at work several hours later.

Amelia Richardson (b. 1830)

A packing case worker who lived and worked on the first floor of 29 Hanbury Street with her grandson. Her son John and a man called John Tyler helped her in her business.

Mrs. Richardson testified that she saw or heard nothing unusual until her grandson told her that a woman had been murdered. Mrs. Richardson went to have a look at the corpse, then returned and remained inside the house until the police arrived. She also stated that prostitutes sometimes took their clients through the gate passage, which was not kept locked, into the yard.

Mr. and Mrs. Copsey

They were cigarette and cigar makers living in the rear of the second story at 29 Hanbury Street, overlooking the murder site.

Like elderly Sarah Cox, they were both asleep at the time of the murder and neither saw nor heard anything. This intelligence they passed on to the press and police.

Mary Hardman

Mrs. Hardman lived with her teenage son, on the ground floor of 29 Hanbury Street, where she kept a cat's meat shop.

She awakened at 6:00 A.M. when she heard some noise and discovered that it was Davis returning with Green and Kent to the backyard. Her son ascertained what was going on and told her, she testified.

Joseph and Thomas Bayley

Owners of Bayley's Packing Case Shop at 23a Hanbury Street, where John Davis ran to summon James Green and James Kent.

Three days following the murder, they discovered a blood-stained piece of paper in their rear yard, but it had not been there when the police searched the yard on the day of the murder.

Edward Stanley

A bricklayer residing, appropriately enough, in Brick Lane, Stanley was a former soldier in the Essex regiment who occasionally had paid for a bed for Annie Chapman and others.

Stanley testified that he had been acquainted with Chapman since the time she had lived in Windsor.

Frederick Stevens

Occupation unknown, Stevens was apparently no relation to William Stevens, who was a resident of Crossingham's Lodging House.

Stevens told the police and newspapers that he and Chapman had a drink together at 12:30 A.M., possibly at Crossingham's, because Stevens went on to say that Chapman stayed at the house until 1:00 A.M., to his knowledge.

Laura Sickings

Laura Sickings was a little girl living at 25 Hanbury Street, who was reported in the press as having made the discovery of a bloodstain on the fence of the backyard where she lived. Inspector

Chandler later examined the stain and determined that it was urine.

Mary Simonds

A nurse at the Whitechapel Infirmary who testified that she and another woman stripped and washed Chapman's body. She further stated that the police did not order her to do this, but whether someone else did or it was on her own initiative is not certain.

Emmanuel Violenia

Violenia was an immigrant boot-finisher living in Hanbury Street who picked John Pizer out of a lineup as the man he had allegedly seen threaten a woman with a knife. When Violenia refused to go to the mortuary to identify Chapman, however, and in the light of his answers to further police questioning, Pizer was released.

THE CASE OF ELIZABETH STRIDE

Matthew Packer

Matthew Packer was an elderly fruiterer who lived at 44 Berner Street, just a few yards from where Elizabeth Stride was murdered. On the night Stride was killed, Packer sold half a pound of black grapes to a man who was walking with her. This was around midnight or a few minutes before, and Packer observed the couple walking and standing around the street until he shut up his shop at 12:30.

In Packer's official statement to the police, which was taken personally by Sir Charles Warren on the afternoon of 4 October, Packer described the man as between twenty-five and thirty years of age, 5 feet 7 inches tall, with a long black coat and wearing a soft felt hat. He also described Stride and the clothes she was wearing. Packer later claimed that he saw the man several times the following month.

Two private detectives, Grand and Batchelor, interviewed Packer, and it was they who discovered the grape stalk in a drain on 2 October. Some witnesses, including Louis Diemschutz, claimed to have seen a grape stalk in Dutfield's Yard on the night of the murder.

The two detectives took Packer to the mortuary, where they first showed him the body of Catherine Eddowes in an attempt to test his reliability. Packer said that he had never seen her, and he was then shown the body of Elizabeth Stride, which he instantly and unhesitatingly identified as the woman he had seen on the date in question.

Packer was written up in the press, and answered all questions put to him honestly and sincerely. Sergeant Stephen White, who interviewed Packer and other residents of Berner Street several hours after the murder, asked him only what he had seen and heard after 12:30. It was the two private detectives who elicited the information about the grape sale.

After the *Evening News* reported the facts garnered by the private detectives, White was sent to requestion Packer by Chief Inspector Henry Moore. Amazingly Packer, a reliable witness with important evidence, was not called to testify at the inquest.

Louis Diemschutz

A salesman of secondhand and imitation jewelry, Louis Diemschutz was also steward of the International Workingmen's Educational Club at 40 Berner Street, to which he was returning in the early morning hours of 30 September, after having been hawking his wares for several hours in Sydenham.

At 1:00 A.M. Diemschutz drove his pony and cart through the wide-open gates of Dutfield's Yard, next to the club. It was his habit to do this. When the pony shied and refused to proceed any further, Diemschutz concluded that the pony was frightened by something and he poked his whip in the darkness. It came into contact with Stride's body. He jumped down and struck a match, thinking that Stride was either asleep or drunk.

He then went on into the club, where he met Morris Eagle and

Isaac Kozebrodsky, fellow club members. The two men returned with Diemschutz to the yard; it was then that they discovered that Stride's throat had been cut and she was dead.

Diemschutz and another club member named Jacobs went for help and returned with Edward Spooner, a horse keeper and trainer whom they met near the Bee Hive public house. Eagle and Kozebrodsky found some policemen whom they brought back a few minutes later.

Diemschutz testified that he took note of a packet of cachous, or breath sweeteners, in the victim's hand as well as some grape stalks lying nearby. He also noticed a flower pinned to Stride's coat.

Police concluded that Diemschutz's arrival had frightened the Ripper, who had time only to slit the victim's throat. Diemschutz later remarked that he believed the Ripper was actually still in the yard somewhere in the darkness, because of the pony's behavior and the very warm temperature of Stride's body. This would seem to be a logical conclusion.

Michael Kidney

Michael Kidney was a waterside laborer living in Dorset Street at the time of Stride's murder. He met Stride in 1885, and the couple lived together on and off for the next three years. Kidney believed Stride to have been well educated, as she spoke without trace of any accent.

In the spring of 1887 Stride brought charges of assault against Kidney, but the case collapsed and was dismissed when she failed to show up in court.

At the time of the murder Kidney had not seen Stride for almost a week, which did not cause him concern, as her periodic absences were not unusual.

The day following Stride's murder, Kidney was seen drunk at a police station. When he asked to see a detective, offering to hunt down the murderer if given cooperation by the police; however, he had no tangible information.

Kidney gave evidence at the inquest and made a statement to the effect that, if he had been the policeman on the beat where Stride had been murdered, he would have killed himself.

Israel Schwartz

Living nearby to Berner Street, Israel Schwartz was walking down the road near Dutfield's Yard sometime just past 12:30 A.M. on 30 September. He reported to the police that he saw a woman, later identified as Stride, talking to a man near the gateway to Dutfield's Yard. The man threw or pushed Stride to the pavement and, noticing Schwartz, cried out "Lipski!" (Lipski was a Polish Jew who had murdered a female lodger in 1887.) A second man, lighting his pipe across the street, chased Schwartz, who eluded his pursuer near a railway arch. Schwartz did not know if the two men knew one another; he did not know them.

Like Packer, Schwartz was not called to testify at the inquest, although he furnished the police with a description of the two men. Stride's assailant, he said, was about 5 feet 5 inches tall, thirty years of age, dark haired and fair complexioned with a brown moustache. The second man, who had ran after him, was approximately 5 feet 9 or 10 inches tall, in his middle thirties, and wearing a black or dark brown overcoat.

Morris Eagle

A Russian Jew living in nearby Commercial Road, Eagle was, like Louis Diemschutz, not only a member of the International Workingmen's Educational Club, but also a seller of cheap jewelry.

Along with Isaac Kozebrodsky, Eagle was told of the presence of the woman in the yard by Diemschutz when the latter came into the club shortly after one o'clock. He went to look at the body, having himself returned to the club only about fifteen minutes previously, after escorting his girlfriend home.

He testified that another club member, Gillman, was with him, singing a folk song, when Diemschutz came in. Eagle then went to find a policeman, and returned with constables Henry Lamb and Edward Collins, whom he had found near Grove Street. When he returned he noticed eight or nine people, including Diemschutz, Jacobs, and Spooner.

Abraham Heahbury

A resident of 28 Berner Street, Heahbury was among the small group of people that gathered at the Stride murder scene in Dutfield's Yard shortly following the discovery of the body by Diemschutz. He may also have been a member of the International Workingmen's Educational Club.

Heahbury, who was seen in the group by Morris Eagle when Eagle returned with the two policemen, later related to a reporter from the *Star* regarding Stride: "In her hand there was a little piece of paper containing five or six cachous."

Isaac Kozebrodsky

Another member of the International Workingmen's Educational Club. Kozebrodsky was upstairs singing a Russian folk song with Eagle and some others when Diemschutz came in with the news. He went down with the other two men to take a look. On discovering that Stride was dead, Eagle went off to get the policemen, with Kozebrodsky apparently following. It is not believed that Kozebrodsky testified at the inquest.

Edward Johnston

A medical assistant to Dr. Blackwell, Johnston testified that he had been summoned from Commercial Road by Police Constable Edward Collins, who came looking for Dr. Blackwell.

Johnston went on ahead, arriving at five minutes past one, and made a brief examination of the body. By this time, ten or twelve people were at the scene. Dr. Blackwell arrived about ten minutes later.

Edward Spooner

A horse trainer and keeper living in Fairclough Street just around the corner to the south of Dutfield's Yard, Spooner testified that

Diemschutz and Jacobs ran up to him shouting "Murder!" as he stood outside the Bee Hive public house at just after one o'clock.

Spooner returned to see the body, and noticed the cachous in Stride's hand—some were also lying on the ground. He also noted that the body was still very warm and blood was still flowing from the throat wound.

J. Best

J. Best was a laborer who recognized Stride in the mortuary as the woman that he had seen at 11:00 P.M. on 29 September in company of a man near the Bricklayer's Arms public house.

Best gave in his evidence a description of the man that is very close to that furnished by Israel Schwartz when he described the man who pushed Stride to the ground.

Elizabeth Tanner (*or* Turner)

A witness at the inquest who provided some incorrect biographical data on Stride. Tanner was the concierge at a lodging house in Flower and Dean Street where Stride had stayed off and on since 1882. She said she paid Stride six shillings to clean rooms in the lodging house on the afternoon of 29 September, and last saw Stride in a pub, the Queen's Head, at 7:00 P.M.

Fanny Mortimer

A woman living with her husband and five children in Berner Street a few yards from the murder site on the same side of the street, Mrs. Mortimer told police that she came outside for some air between 12:30 and 12:45 A.M. She must have just missed all the passersby, for she stated she saw nobody except Leon Goldstein, who was walking down the street with some empty matchboxes. A press report quotes her as having heard several noises, but she saw nothing and was not called as a witness.

Joseph Lave

Lave was a Russian immigrant who was living at the Working-men's Club at 40 Berner Street on the night of the killing.

He gave evidence that he went outside for a smoke about 12:40 A.M., passing through Dutfield's Yard, which was in total darkness. He was positive that no one was in the yard at that time, as he had to grope his way along the wall in order to get to the entrance, and would have bumped into anything that was there (including the body).

Leon Goldstein

A resident of Christian Street, he was passing through Berner Street the night of Stride's murder carrying a little black bag. On 1 October, Goldstein became aware of the fact that Mrs. Mortimer had seen a man walking in the area carrying such a bag, and he went to a nearby police station in Leman Street, identifying himself as that man.

Thomas Coram

A witness who testified at the Stride inquest that he had found a bloodstained knife in Whitechapel Road. The knife had a ten-inch blade and was very sharp. The remarkable thing is that the police knew Coram had found the knife twenty-four hours before Stride was killed; one therefore wonders why he was called as a witness at all. It was ascertained that the knife could not have caused the mutilations.

James Brown

Brown saw Elizabeth Stride and a man near the Board School in Fairclough Street about five minutes or so before she was seen by Israel Schwartz. He gave evidence that the man was about 5 feet 7 inches tall and wore a long overcoat. Brown overheard a few snippets of conversation between the couple but noticed nothing out of the ordinary in regard to the behavior or appearance of either party.

Philip Kranz (1859–1922)

A Russian Jew who gave evidence at Stride's inquest, Kranz had a newspaper office behind 40 Berner Street and was there editing the paper when Stride was killed.

On his way out, just after 1:00 A.M., he heard a commotion in Dutfield's Yard as he passed by and saw the body and a small crowd of people milling around. The police arrived a few minutes later, he said.

Catherine Lane

Another resident of 32 Flower and Dean Street, cleaning woman Catherine Lane gave evidence that she had known Stride since 1882.

Lane said that Stride had been staying at the lodging house for several days, and she last saw her at about 8:00 P.M. on 29 September.

Charles Letchford

The brother of Mrs. Mortimer and living in Berner Street at No. 39, Letchford told the police that he had walked down the street at about 12:30 A.M., at which time he noticed nothing unusual. Not called as an inquest witness, he nevertheless was interviewed by the *Manchester Guardian,* where he reiterated his sister's story.

William Marshall (b. 1841)

A boot maker and inquest witness, Marshall stated that he was outside of 64 Berner Street close to midnight when he observed

Stride (whom he later identified in the mortuary) in company with a man 5 feet 6 inches tall and wearing a black coat. This may have been the man seen by Gardner and Best in Settles Street. Marshall observed the couple heading in the direction of Packer's fruiterer's shop.

William West

West gave evidence to the effect that he had passed through Dutfield's Yard at about 12:30 A.M. on 30 September and noticed nothing out of the ordinary. A printer by profession, West went to the newspaper office to see Philip Kranz and to return some literature. He then went to the International Workingmen's Educational Club.

Charles Preston

Preston was a barber who lived at 32 Flower and Dean Street. His evidence consisted of relating that he had last seen Stride in the lodging house kitchen on the evening of the twenty-ninth, at about 6:30 P.M. He also related some of the false background that Stride had given him.

Barnett Kentorrich

Kentorrich lived at 38 Berner Street, Dutfield's Yard separating his residence from the International Workingmen's Educational Club. When questioned during the house-to-house search by the police, he told Sergeant Stephen White that he had been asleep and heard nothing until White got him out of bed.

Thomas Bates

The night watchman of the lodging house at 32 Flower and Dean Street, Bates described Stride at the inquest as a cheerful soul, referring to her by the nickname of "Long Liz."

He added that he saw Stride for the last time around 7:30 P.M. on 29 September, stating that he noticed nothing unusual in her demeanor or behavior.

Mary Malcolm

A possible hoaxer or mental defective, Mary Malcolm, upon learning of the murder told the police that she had ''a vision'' that the murdered woman was her sister, going so far as to identify the body at the mortuary as the same, despite the admonishings of Coroner Baxter. The story blew up in her face when her sister, Elizabeth Stokes, showed up at the inquest. Apparently no charges were brought against Malcolm.

Elizabeth Stokes

Mrs. Stokes was upset to read in the newspapers that her sister had identified the body of Stride as that of herself, and did not care for being referred to as a prostitute. Her only contribution to the inquest was to say that she was alive and well. Stokes had been in and out of several insane asylums, but evidence suggests that it was her sister, Mary Malcolm, who should have gone before the Lunacy Commission.

THE CASE OF CATHERINE EDDOWES

John Kelly

Irish porter John Kelly met Catherine Eddowes the year after the death of her husband, in 1881, and lived with her for the next seven years, lastly at Flower and Dean (''Flowery Dean'') Street. The couple seemed to have been happy together, and John Kelly was described by those who knew him as an introspective and unobtrusive sort.

During the month of September 1888, Kelly and Eddowes went to Kent to pick hops. Apparently they did not fare very well, and returned to London on 29 September, where they took separate lodgings. After settling in, the couple met at Cooney's Lodging House, where Kelly had taken a room. Since they were once again out of money, Kelly gave Eddowes an extra pair of his boots, which she pawned. This provided them with at least enough money for a good meal and quite a few drinks.

Later that same day that money, too, was gone, and Eddowes had the idea of traveling to see her married daughter in order to get some more. That was the last Kelly saw of her until he viewed her body in Golden Lane Mortuary.

Kelly testified that he came forward when he read in a newspaper that a pawn ticket in the name of Birrell, one of their friends, was found among the deceased's possessions.

Joseph Lawende

A tobacco salesman by trade, Joseph Lawende was also a member of the Imperial Club, located just around the corner from Mitre Square.

He gave evidence that at 1:30 or so on the morning of 30 September, in company with friends Harry Harris and Joseph Levy, he observed Eddowes and a man standing in the entrance to Mitre Square, apparently sheltering there under an archway from a light rain that was falling. Lawende later recognized Eddowes's body in Golden Lane Mortuary.

Lawende was the only one of the three who got a good look at the man, whose appearance did not seem other than ordinary to Lawende. He nevertheless provided the police with a description: age, about thirty; height 5 feet 7 inches, fair complexion, brown moustache; dress, salt-and-pepper coat, a red kerchief, and peaked cloth cap. Lawende described the man as being of sailorly bearing.

Sir Henry Smith evidently thought that Lawende's evidence was important, as he kept the press away from him until the time of the inquest. A city solicitor asked at the inquest, for unknown reasons, that Lawende not give the man's description at that time.

Joseph Levy (1841–1892?)

Levy was an Aldgate butcher who testified that, along with Lawende and Harris, he saw Eddowes with a man outside Duke Street near Mitre Square. Levy did not take any special notice of the couple, but remarked that the square should be watched, adding, "I don't like going home by myself when I see these sort of characters about. I'm off."

At the same time that Harris was interviewed by the *Evening News,* they asked Levy for his comments. The article was published on 9 October. The press seemed to infer from Levy's attitude and answers to their questions that he knew or saw more than he was telling.

Harry Harris

In company with Joseph Lawende and Joseph Levy, Harris, a furniture salesman, left the Imperial Club just after 1:30 A.M.

Harris gave an interview to the *Evening News* a week or so after the murder, stating that he and his companions saw a woman and man right after they left the club near Church Passage, the entrance to Mitre Square. He also said that he paid no particular attention to these people and doubted if he would be able to recognize them again.

George Morris

A former police officer and the watchman at Kearley & Tonge's Warehouse, Morris was on duty at 1:45 when Police Constable Edward Watkins, who knew Morris, came for help. Watkins had discovered the body. Morris testified that Watkins had said, "For God's sake, mate, come to assist me," to which Morris asked, "What's the matter?" Watkins then replied, "Oh dear, here's another woman cut up to pieces." Morris returned to Mitre Square to look at the body, then went off blowing his whistle, which was answered by P.C. James Harvey.

Annie Phillips (b. 1865)

The twenty-three-year-old married daughter of Catherine Eddowes, a resident of Southwark, testified as to her mother's character.

Phillips said she had not seen her mother for about two years—which was all right with her, as Eddowes had been a sponge on her family. They naturally did not keep in touch with her, and in fact avoided her.

From this evidence, it would seem clear that Eddowes was unsuccessful in locating her daughter and must have found the money she got drunk on elsewhere.

James Blenkinsop

A railway night watchman in St. James Place near Mitre Square, Blenkinsop was quoted in the *Star* the day after the murder as having seen a well-dressed man nearby at 1:30. The man approached Blenkinsop and asked him if he had seen a couple pass by recently. Blenkinsop told the man that he had, but took no particular notice of where they were going.

Blenkinsop was not called as an inquest witness, and it is uncertain whether police made further inquiries regarding his statement.

Frederick W. Wilkinson

The deputy at Cooney's Lodging House, located at 55-56 Flower and Dean Street, Wilkinson testified at the inquest that he had seen John Kelly and Catherine Eddowes together at the lodging house in the late morning and early afternoon of 29 of September. He did not see Eddowes after that time.

George Clapp

A resident of Mitre Square (No. 5), Clapp testified that he was a caretaker, and furthermore that he had heard nothing during the night of the murder. Clapp's window looked out on the square itself.

Frederick Foster

A surveyor who brought blueprints to the Eddowes inquest, he also made drawings (which were later published) of the body and its injuries as he saw in the mortuary. The blueprints showed not only Mitre Square, but also Goulston Street, where graffiti was discovered by P.C. Long.

THE CASE OF MARY JANE KELLY

George Hutchinson (1866–1938)

Hutchinson was a resident of the Peabody Buildings in Commercial Street, and was acquainted with Mary Kelly for about three years. He occasionally gave her a shilling.

He saw Kelly at about 2:00 A.M. in Thrawl Street on the day of her murder, 9 November 1888. She asked him for sixpence, but he told her he had no money, to which Kelly replied, "Good morning, I must go and find some money."

Kelly walked away and was almost immediately joined by a man near Commercial and Flower and Dean Streets. Hutchinson did not like the look of the man, who carried a little black bag and tried to avert his face from Hutchinson, who nonetheless got a good look at him. Hutchinson later said the man "looked at me stern."

Hutchinson followed the couple at a discreet distance into Dorset Street past the Queen's Head public house, where they stood for three or four minutes outside the entrance to Miller's Court. The man put his arm on Kelly's shoulder and she responded by kissing him. They then went into the court itself, out of Hutchinson's view.

Hutchinson remained outside the court for about three-quarters of an hour; he was most likely the stoutish man in the wideawake hat seen by Sarah Lewis. Finally, Hutchinson got tired of hanging about and went home.

Hutchinson later provided the police with a very accurate and precise description of the man. About 5 feet 6 inches tall and in his middle thirties, the man had a brown moustache curled and waxed at the tips, dark hair, and a light complexion. He wore a long, dark coat with astrakhan collar and cuffs, dark jacket and trousers, and carried a small, shiny black bag of American cloth.

His dark hat was turned down in the middle; he wore black boots with white buttons and spats, a light-colored waistcoat, and a black tie.

Particular items of jewelry noticed by Hutchinson included a gold watch chain with a red stone seal, and a horseshoe tiepin. He also described the man as being of Jewish appearance. The police changed this last remark to "foreign-looking," as they did not want any anti-Semitic problems like those resulting from the "Leather Apron" scare or the "Juwes" (see Chapter 4, "Politicians and Police," "Sir Charles Warren" entry for further discussion) message.

Hutchinson was very observant, and it is absolutely amazing that he was not called as an inquest witness. Some authors and researchers have theorized that Hutchinson was excluded due to a cover-up. A more likely explanation is that Roderick MacDonald, the coroner who handled the Kelly inquest, was just plain stupid. It has been argued that Wynne Baxter should have been in charge of Kelly's inquest—even the jurors thought so. When one juror asked MacDonald why Baxter was not in charge, seeing that the murder was committed in Baxter's district, MacDonald angrily snapped that the body now lay in a place that came under *his* jurisdiction. In any event, MacDonald grossly mishandled the proceedings, concluding it so fast that Hutchinson's important evidence, as well as other witnesses and evidence, were never allowed into the record.

John McCarthy (b. 1851)

The landlord of Miller's Court, who kept a chandler's shop at 27 Dorset Street. Miller's Court was locally known by the nickname "McCarthy's Rents."

At 10:45 A.M. on Friday, 9 November, McCarthy sent Thomas Bowyer to 13 Miller's Court to collect the rent money that Kelly

owed him. A few minutes later Bowyer came racing back to tell
McCarthy what he had found. McCarthy returned with Bowyer to
the court and looked through the window. What he saw shocked
him.

McCarthy next went to Commercial Road Police Station, where
he found Inspector Walter Beck, who returned with him to the court,
accompanied by several police sergeants and constables.

For the next several hours nothing happened, as the police
expected the arrival of the bloodhounds Burgho and Barnaby, but
when it became clear that the dogs were not coming, McCarthy
smashed in the door with an axe handle on Superintendent
Arnold's orders.

McCarthy later expressed in the press deep shock and sadness
at the murder, adding that some of his tenants had moved away
from Miller's Court following the atrocity.

Thomas Bowyer

Residing in Dorset Street at No. 37, Bowyer, a former member of
the British army who had served in India, did odd jobs for
chandler's shop owner and landlord John McCarthy.

On the morning of 9 November 1888, McCarthy sent Bowyer
to 13 Miller's Court to collect the rent money from Mary Kelly,
who was now some weeks in arrears. When Bowyer received no
response to his knocking (he also tried the door but it was locked),
he reached through the broken windowpane, pushed aside the
curtain, and saw the carnage inside. Bowyer then ran and fetched
McCarthy, who returned with him to the scene and also looked
through the window. McCarthy then went to the police station
while Bowyer remained at Miller's Court.

Elizabeth Prater

Mrs. Prater testified that she lived in the room directly above
Kelly in Miller's Court, and that she had known the deceased
some five or six months.

She arrived home on the day of the murder about 1:00 A.M. and
did not see or hear anything suspicious or unusual.

About four o'clock in the morning, Diddles, Mrs. Prater's kitten, awakened her by walking over her head. It was a few minutes later that Prater heard a cry of "Murder!" to which she did not pay much attention as cries of this nature were common enough in the neighborhood. Mrs. Prater went back to sleep.

Sarah Lewis

A laundress who testified at the inquest, Sarah Lewis was visiting the Keylers at 2 Miller's Court on the night of the murder.

Arriving at the court at about 2:30 A.M., she noticed a man with a wideawake black hat, apparently Hutchinson, keeping a watch on the court entrance. She also saw a man and woman walking along the street, but could not be sure if Kelly was the woman.

Lewis also told of an encounter she herself had had a few days beforehand in which she encountered a man carrying a black bag, but this does not appear to be relevant to the case.

Julia Venturney

A laundress living at No. 1 Miller's Court, Venturney testified that she had seen Mary Kelly break the window at No. 13 a few weeks before the murder, apparently while drunk.

She knew Kelly and Joseph Barnett, as well as other of their acquaintances. Venturney further stated that she had been at home on the night of the murder and sleeping, and therefore heard or saw nothing.

Maria Harvey

A prostitute who sometimes shared lodgings with Mary Kelly in Miller's Court, Harvey had been the reason that Joe Barnett had argued with Kelly and subsequently moved out. He disapproved of Kelly keeping company with Harvey and other prostitutes.

Harvey testified that she had been drinking on the evening of 8 November with Kelly and was with her at Miller's Court until about 7:30 P.M., at which time Barnett arrived and she left.

Mary Ann Cox

An inquest witness, Cox lived at 5 Miller's Court and gave evidence that she saw Kelly in the company of a blotchy-complexioned man with a carroty moustache who was carrying a pail of beer. This was at Miller's Court around midnight. She went on to say that she listened to Kelly singing for a while, and several hours later heard footsteps going away from Miller's Court.

Maurice Lewis

A tailor who lived in Dorset Street, Maurice Lewis told the newspapers that he had seen Kelly with Barnett in the Horn of Plenty public house on the eve of the murder. He also thought he saw her about 10:00 A.M. the following day, which is probably why he was considered an unreliable witness, not taken seriously, or called to the inquest, as Kelly had been dead for hours by that time.

Mrs. Kennedy

An informant who went to visit her parents in Miller's Court at the time of the murder, Mrs. Kennedy told Inspector Frederick Abberline that she arrived at the court at about 3:15 A.M. and noticed a drunken man talking to a woman nearby.

She also stated that she heard a cry of "Murder!" sometime around 4:00 A.M. Whether the woman she saw upon arriving at the court was Kelly cannot be verified.

Caroline Maxwell

A witness at the inquest, Mrs. Maxwell stated she had seen Mary Kelly a few times but did not know her. She went on to say that she thought she saw Kelly near Miller's Court at 8:30 A.M. on the ninth, but medical evidence proved that this could not have been so. Most likely she saw Kelly the day before—Maxwell already stated that she did not know Kelly very well. Allowing Maxwell's so-called evidence and leaving out Hutchinson was just part of the foofaraw of the farcical MacDonald-orchestrated inquest.

Lizzie Albrook (b. 1868)

Lizzie Albrook was a young acquaintance of Mary Kelly who worked in a Dorset Street lodging house and lived in Miller's Court.

Lizzie told the press that Kelly often warned her not to turn to a life of prostitution as she, Kelly, had done. Albrook last saw Kelly at Miller's Court on 8 November with Joe Barnett at a quarter to eight.

Mr. and Mrs. Keyler

Residents of Miller's Court, the Keylers were visited by Sarah Lewis on the night of the Kelly murder.

When questioned by the police, they said they knew Mary Kelly, but neither saw nor heard anything of a suspicious nature.

3. SUSPECTS

The following is a list of those persons who were suspected by the police of 1888 or have been proposed through the years by various authors.

As the reader will know, there have been many fictional accounts written about the Whitechapel murderer, and equally fictitious or nonexistent suspects. The purpose of this book is to deal with the facts of the case; therefore, one can take for granted that all those listed in this section were real people who existed at the time of the murders. The unnamed are not included (i.e., slaughterman, mysterious doctor, etc.).

I beg the reader's indulgence if I have included anyone too farfetched in this section. For example, Joseph Barnett, who should rightly be found in the "Witnesses" chapter, is included here only because an author has seen fit to make him the killer in his book, even though the evidence is gossamer-thin and can be refuted. In fact, all the cases against these suspects can be broken down to some degree. Most authors have taken facts and applied or tailored them to suit their own purposes.

James Maybrick (1838–1889)

A Liverpool cotton merchant, James Maybrick came to the fore as a suspect in 1993 when Smith Gryphon of London published a controversial sixty-three-page document allegedly written by Maybrick and purporting to be the diary of Jack the Ripper. Experts have not been able to determine or agree upon the authenticity of the diary, which nevertheless is quite fascinating.

Although living in Liverpool, Maybrick supposedly rented rooms near Whitechapel at the time of the murders. A fairly prosperous man of respectable appearance, Maybrick was an arsenic eater and hypochondriac who was ultimately poisoned by his wife in May

1889. The diary begins in March 1888, and continues until 3 May 1889, about a week before Maybrick was murdered.

Many details in the diary appear to be authentic, but there are a great many questions one would like answered. At the diary's conclusion, the writer, who signs himself Jack the Ripper, assures that it will be placed in a safe place where it will be easily found. Why then did it take more than a century to come to light? The owner of the diary, a publican named Michael Barrett, states that a friend gave it to him with no explanation. Since the friend just happened to have died, there is now no evidence of the provenance of the diary, or where it has been for over a hundred years.

By coincidence, very shortly before the book was published, a watch was brought to the attention of the publisher; it supposedly had the name James Maybrick scratched into its case, along with the initials of the five East End victims. The watch also had a date of 1846 inscribed upon it.

Maybrick's whereabouts at the time of the murders has not been established; some have theorized that his wife murdered him because she knew he was the Ripper, although it seems more probable that her affairs with various men were the motive.

George Hutchinson may well have seen the Ripper, as perhaps did Israel Schwartz; both men described the suspect as in his thirties—Maybrick was fifty, and research into his appearance indicated he looked his age, if not older, due to his drug taking and illnesses. Also, there is no evidence to suggest that Maybrick possessed any surgical, medical, or anatomical skills or knowledge.

One also wonders, since Maybrick did not die until more than six months after the Kelly murder, why there were no further killings. The diary definitely holds the attention, however, and James Maybrick can now be added to the long list of Jack the Ripper suspects.

Prince Albert Victor, Duke of Clarence and Avondale (1864–1892)

The grandson of Queen Victoria and son of the future King Edward VII, Prince Albert Victor, or "Eddy" as he was known to his intimates, was first proposed as Jack the Ripper in an article by Dr. Thomas Stowell (1885–1970).

Stowell's basis for this was a reference in the papers of Sir William Gull, the royal court physician, in which Gull informed ''a certain person'' not named that his son was dying of syphilis of the brain.

The theory here is that the prince had some years previously contracted syphilis from a prostitute and when he realized this he decided to murder women of this profession. Stowell later denied that he had suggested the prince was the Ripper—in fact he refers to his suspect only as ''S.'' By an amazing coincidence Stowell dropped dead the day after he wrote this article, subsequently published in the *Times* of London. Unfortunately, Stowell's family destroyed all his notes.

Author Frank Spiering also names the prince as Jack the Ripper in his book *Prince Jack,* a blend of fact and fiction. Spiering and others would have done well, however, to check the prince's movements and whereabouts on the dates of the killings. When Nichols was killed on 31 August, the prince was in Yorkshire at a house party; he was in York at the Cavalry Barracks on 8 September when Chapman was murdered. The night of the double event (Stride and Eddowes), 30 September, he was in Scotland where he had been since the twenty-seventh of the month and at Sandringham to celebrate his father's birthday when Kelly was killed (in fact he was there 2–12 November).

The prince provides the motive for the murders in theories that revolve around Sir William Gull, Lord Randolph Churchill, John Netley, Walter Sickert, Freemasonry, and conspiracy.

Montague J. Druitt (1857–1888)

A well-known cricketer, failed barrister, and dismissed tutor, Montague Druitt was a suspect, at least after the killings— brought to light as early as 1894 in a memorandum by Sir Melville MacNaghten. MacNaghten did, however, mistranscribe several facts: Druitt was thirty-one, not forty-one; a barrister and not a doctor; his suicide date was the first week of December and not 10 November as MacNaghten stated in his memoirs.

There was insanity in the Druitt family, and MacNaghten thought him to be ''sexually insane.'' Druitt's movements cannot definitely be verified at the time of the murders, but it has been ascertained that he was miles away playing cricket a few hours after three of the murders occurred. This makes it appear unlikely that he had anything to do with them.

In Druitt's case there has been a great deal of conjecture and hearsay regarding his family, relatives, and background. One thing that is known for certain is that Druitt's body was pulled out of the Thames by waterman Henry Winslade on 31 December 1888. The inquest, which took place two days later, returned a verdict of suicide while the balance of the mind was disturbed, and is greatly supported by the facts.

Apparently Druitt had been dead almost a month when his body was found, and some believe that this proves he was the killer. They reason that the murders stopped when Druitt died, and this is supposed to be damning evidence against him. Almost certainly it is just a coincidence.

Sir William Withey Gull (1816–1890)

The royal physician, Sir William Gull, has become, especially recently, one of the most popular suspects as Jack the Ripper. Gull certainly had the surgical skill and medical knowledge necessary to perform the mutilations, but one wonders how vigorous a seventy-two-year-old man who had recently had a stroke would have been.

Several authors have been proponents of theories involving Gull, usually with the aid of coachman John Netley and sometimes artist Walter Sickert. There are, of course, a number of variations—one including Lord Randolph Churchill not only in the conspiracy but also in the actual murders.

The Gull theory was the basis for two excellent motion pictures: the 1979 British-Canadian *Murder by Decree* (although the names of Gull and Netley have been changed) and the 1988 British-made television film *Jack the Ripper* starring Michael Caine as Abberline and Ray McAnally as Sir William Gull. Gull was the suspect named by Sir Peter Ustinov in a TV documentary marking the one hundredth anniversary of the murders.

The basic plot goes like this: Prince Albert Victor sires an illegitimate child. Mary Kelly, a friend of the artist Sickert, becomes nurse to the baby. After the child's mother is kidnapped and lobotomized by Gull, Kelly and four other prostitutes attempt to blackmail the government.

Gull gets involved on orders or possibly by implication by Lord Salisbury or other government officials. This is aided by a police cover-up; most of the principals are high-ranking Freemasons. The murders are committed according to Masonic rite, the victims are killed, the downfall of the monarchy and government is averted, as is possible civil war.

All this is quite fascinating and entertaining, if highly speculative and imaginative. Although Gull is a popular suspect, he is an improbable one.

James Kenneth Stephen (1859–1892)

Lawyer, poet, Cambridge don, and former tutor to Prince Albert Victor, Stephen first came up as a suspect in Michael Harrison's book about the prince. Harrison did not like the prince as a suspect, so he tried to find someone else who fit the "facts." This was Stephen.

The case against Stephen is very improbable and shaky. Aside from the fact that his surname begins with the letter *S* (Stowell had referred to his suspect simply as "S"), the only other facts against Stephen are that he was a known misogynist and sadist, and had suffered a violent blow to the head around 1885. The resulting brain damage finally sent Stephen to an asylum, where he was confined until his death in 1892.

Stephen was a patient of Sir William Gull, and Harrison believes that Stephen committed the murders on certain royal anniversaries or birthdays. Harrison also mistakenly ascribes ten murders to the killer.

George Chapman (1865–1903)

Polish-born Severin Klosowski emigrated to London, later changing his name to George Chapman. He was a Whitechapel barber's surgeon and hairdresser living in the East End when the murders occurred.

There is no evidence as to his exact whereabouts at the times of the murders, but there are a number of reasons that he was suspected, even if they can be discounted.

In addition to having some skill with the knife, Chapman also matched the description of men seen by various witnesses and apparently had a doppelganger in Dr. Alexander Pedachenko.

Inspector Abberline is supposed to have remarked to George Godley, ''I see you've got Jack the Ripper at last,'' when Godley arrested Chapman for a series of murders by poison some years later. Chapman was found guilty and hanged on 7 April 1903.

Abberline stated his reasons for the assumption that Chapman was the Ripper: When Chapman came to London, the murders began; when he left, they stopped. He matched witnesses descriptions of the suspect, and had medical training. All this could be said of hundreds, if not thousands, of men in London at that time. While Chapman was a murderer to be sure, he was a poisoner, and therefore the case against him as the Ripper is weak.

Michael Ostrog (b. 1833)

Russian-born swindler, thief, and confidence trickster, long in the United Kingdom where his record of offenses is varied, lengthy, and well documented, going back more than twenty-five years prior to the Whitechapel atrocities.

Well spoken and of upper-class appearance and manners, Ostrog nonetheless made a career out of getting into one sort of criminal activity after another, and spent a considerable period in jail on and off over the years, as well in as the occasional lunatic asylum.

During the Jack the Ripper murders, the police were looking for Ostrog for failure to appear and violations relating to his probation. Sir Melville MacNaghten named Ostrog as one of his three suspects, stating that Ostrog was a bad lot and habitually carried sharp knives on his person.

Dr. Alexander Pedachenko (c. 1857–1909)

Russian secret agent and look-alike of George Chapman, Pedachenko's inclusion as a Jack the Ripper suspect is highly speculative.

According to the theories, Pedachenko was allegedly a secret agent of the Ochrana, the Russian secret police, who was sent to London to commit the murders in order to discredit the British police. Pedachenko's involvement was supposedly mentioned in papers written by Rasputin, and the whole story seems highly unlikely and imaginative. The Ochrana is supposed to have assisted Pedachenko to escape from London and back to Russia, where several years later he was caught attempting a murder. He was then put into a lunatic asylum where he eventually died.

Lord Randolph Churchill (1849–1894)

The conservative statesman and father of Sir Winston Churchill has recently been suggested in several books as a suspect in the murders. In *The Whitechapel Murders* by Edward B. Hanna, a fact-based novel featuring fictional detective Sherlock Holmes, and Melvin Fairclough's *Ripper and the Royals,* Churchill is described as the highest-ranking Freemason in England in 1888. It was he, along with Sir William Gull, possibly aided by Walter Sickert and John Netley, who committed the murders.

This theory ties in with the conspiracy theory put forth by Stephen Knight; the motive behind it all is the protection of the monarchy and the good name of Prince Albert Victor. Joseph Sickert, son of Walter, asserts that there is evidence of this in a diary supposedly penned by Inspector Frederick Abberline in 1896.

Walter R. Sickert (1860–1942)

A well-known artist, Sickert has been mentioned as a suspect in several books and articles, not on his own, but in connection with the Freemasonry conspiracy and Sir William Gull.

There are a great many variations on the theory, but basically it involved Sickert as a friend of Prince Albert Victor, introducing him to a girl named Annie Crook in Cleveland Street. The prince was supposed to have sired a daughter on Crook, and in order to protect the prince and prevent a scandal, Mary Kelly (and several others) were killed because they attempted to blackmail the royal family. Kelly was alleged to have been a nurse to the baby, telling several of her contemporaries of its existence.

Some theorists have intimated that there are hidden messages in Sickert's artwork, and that since he described the victims' injuries in such detail he must have seen the bodies.

Dr. Thomas Neill Cream (1850–1892)

Scottish-born Cream had a varied career in England, Canada, and the United States. He had medical practices in several towns, and first got into trouble performing illegal abortions. One of his patients died, and he was arrested.

The subject of the excellent book *The Gentleman from Chicago,* by John Cashman, Cream was apparently serving a term in prison in Joliet, Illinois, in 1888 at the time of the Ripper killings. It has been suggested that he either bribed his way out of prison or had a double that took his place, and therefore would have been able to be in the East End of London at the right time.

In any case, Cream poisoned several prostitutes in Lambeth in 1891 and 1892. His morbid fascination with writing letters of blackmail and taunting the police helped to snare him. As he was being hanged on 15 November 1892, Cream uttered the words, ''I am Jack the . . .''

Frederick Bailey Deeming (1842–1892)

A pipe fitter and plumber by trade, Deeming was also a con man who murdered at least two wives and several children in both England and in Australia. It is believed that he was in prison at the time of the murders in Whitechapel.

Deeming was charged with the murder of his wife in Melbourne, Australia, in 1892, and while on trial confessed to being Jack the Ripper. Meanwhile in England, the bodies of his first wife and their four children were found cemented under the floor in Deeming's former residence at Rainhill, near Liverpool. It was reported that there was a message written on the back door that ''Jack the Ripper lived here.''

Deeming wrote his memoirs while awaiting execution, asserting that, while not guilty of the crime for which he was incarcerated, he was in fact Jack the Ripper. There is a plaster death mask

of Deeming in Scotland Yard's Black Museum that is identified
as that of Jack the Ripper.

Frederick Chapman (1851–1888)

A surgeon and former army doctor, Chapman was arrested on 1
October 1888 by Police Constable Robert Spicer. Spicer wrote in
1931 that he had gotten into trouble for arresting Chapman, a
respectable Brixton doctor. Spicer was convinced that he had
captured the Ripper.

The reasons for Chapman's arrest were that he was talking to a
known prostitute, had blood on his cuffs, and was carrying a bag
(probably his doctor's bag). Spicer regretted that Chapman was
not made to open the bag.

John Pizer (1850–1897)

John Pizer, a Polish Jew and boot-finisher, was actually arrested
by Sergeant William Thicke at his home in Mulberry Street on the
morning of 10 September 1888. This followed the "Leather
Apron" scare created by the discovery of John Richardson's
soaked leather apron in the backyard at 29 Hanbury Street, where
Annie Chapman was killed.

Pizer was in the habit of wearing a leather apron as well as using
a number of long, sharp knives. Emmanuel Violenia stated that he
has seen Pizer (whom he knew as "Leather Apron") in Hanbury
Street at the time of the murder arguing with a woman. But when
Violenia refused to go to the mortuary to look at Chapman's body,
and in light of his further answers to police questioning, they began
to distrust Violenia, and Pizer was released. Pizer later won several
lawsuits against newspapers that had libeled him.

John W. Sanders (1862–1901)

Sanders was a medical student whose name came up in connection with the Ripper killings in correspondence between Sir
Charles Warren and Inspector Fred Abberline.

All that is known for certain about Sanders is that he was a medical student at London Hospital who became ill and was placed in an asylum in the early 1880s. A medical memorandum in 1887 showed that his condition had increasingly worsened and he was given to fits of violence.

Apparently Sanders was in a Virginia Water lunatic asylum at the time of the murders, although police reports mention that inquiries were made, without result, as to the whereabouts of "John Sanders, an insane medical student."

Joseph Barnett (1858–1927)

Joseph Barnett should be listed in Chapter 2 ("Witnesses"), save that author Paul Harrison alleges that Barnett was the Ripper.

Barnett was a riverside laborer and market porter, and Harrison states, quite stupidly, that Barnett possessed the necessary skills to perform the mutilations because he knew how to gut fish at Billingsgate Fish Market. This is asinine logic. When cleaning a fish, one simply guts it; a child can do that. One does not remove the fish's liver, kidneys, etc., individually.

Harrison suggests that Barnett's motive was to frighten Mary Kelly (with whom he lived) off the streets, but Harrison fails to take into account that Barnett had to wake up early to go to work, and would have been sleeping when the killings took place. If he had gone out at all (and then returned with blood on him or his clothes), Kelly would have become suspicious. Harrison further gives as "evidence" the fact that he met someone named Barnett who told him Joseph Barnett was the killer.

Since the police at the time minutely examined Barnett's clothing immediately following the Kelly murder, as well as questioning him for four hours, we can be sure they were satisfied that he had nothing to do with the murders.

John Netley (1860–1903)

A coachman and alleged coconspirator variously with Sir William Gull, Lord Randolph Churchill, Walter Sickert, etc., Netley owned his own coach and supposedly drove Prince Albert Victor on occasion. It is unlikely that Netley was a Freemason, but he is involved in the conspiracy theory according to Joseph Sickert, Stephen Knight, and others.

Joseph Sickert believed that the murders were done in Netley's cab, which is most unlikely. In the scores of witnesses' testimonies, no mention of a cab is found; at that time and in that area cabs were uncommon and would have been heard as well as seen. Some researchers, however, give credence to Netley as a suspect—it would be unlikely for Joseph Sickert to have heard of this little-known man. In 1903, Netley was killed, thrown from his coach when it struck a curb, the wheel crushing his head.

Aaron Kosminski (1864–1919)

Kosminski was a Polish Jew who escaped the pogroms and came to England in 1882, working in the East End as a hairdresser.

Sir Melville MacNaghten names Kosminski as one of the three suspects in his memorandum, stating that he "became insane owing to solitary vices." MacNaghten also stated that Kosminski was very similar in appearance to a suspect that had been seen by a constable near Mitre Square at the time of the Eddowes murder.

Sir Robert Anderson as well as Chief Inspector Donald Swanson seemed to indicate Kosminski as a suspect—Swanson noting the name Kosminski in the margin of a page of a copy of Anderson's autobiography. Anderson did not name the suspect, but it was likely Kosminski.

Dr. Robert Donstan Stephenson (b. 1841)

Also known as Roslyn D'Onston, Stephenson, a former chemist and medical student, was a theorist who also dabbled in the occult. He was put forward as a suspect by occultist Aleister Crowley (1875–1947), who claimed to possess some bloodstained ties having belonged to Stephenson.

Crowley further asserted that Stephenson was a master magician who had simply "disappeared" after each murder. The purpose, Crowley said, was to kill the victims in places that formed a cross when drawn on a map. This seems quite absurd, but author Melvin Harris believes Stephenson to be the Ripper, due to the fact that he fit all the known requirements, but then, so did many others.

G. Wentworth Bell Smith

A Canadian trust agent, Smith came to London on business in 1888 and remained until the following year. He stayed in lodgings with a couple, Mr. and Mrs. Edward Callaghan.

Smith behaved strangely; he was often out at odd times, talked to himself, wrote copious religious-based notes, and had a loathing of prostitutes, who Smith said should be exterminated.

After he changed addresses at the height of the Ripper scare, Callaghan became convinced that Smith was the killer, reporting his suspicions of Smith to the police. Their attitude at the time seems to indicate that they thought Smith was merely an eccentric.

Dr. William Westcott (1848–1925)

A Freemason of high rank and coroner for West London during the Jack the Ripper atrocities, Westcott was also cofounder of a pseudo-Masonic occult society called the Order of the Golden Dawn. Also the author of a score of books dealing with the occult, Westcott came up as a suspect in articles by Christopher Smith and Ron Mabers, who believed that the murders were occult ritualistic sacrifices.

There is no tangible or reasonable argument for suspecting Westcott's involvement.

Joseph Isenschmidt (b. 1848)

A butcher by trade, Isenschmidt was brought to the attention of the police by a doctor who treated Isenschmidt for a breakdown and thought he might be the Ripper.

Isenschmidt bragged that he was ''Leather Apron'' after the Chapman murder. A man had been seen wandering about with blood on his hands (if Isenschmidt, not unusual considering his profession) and Inspector Abberline was convinced Isenschmidt was the man.

Unfortunately, Isenschmidt's condition grew worse, and he was confined to an asylum once more. At least his confinement cleared him of further suspicion; the last three murders were committed while he was in the asylum.

Nathan Kaminsky (b. 1865)

Sometimes confused with Aaron Cohen, Kaminsky was a Jewish boot maker living in Whitechapel during 1888. Author Martin Fido suggests he was "Leather Apron" and fits the necessary criteria for being Jack the Ripper.

The Kaminsky information is highly conjectural and speculative, and involves the theory that either the City of London Police or the Metropolitan Police knew Kaminsky was the Ripper, keeping the information from the other force, while at the same time keeping Kaminsky under surveillance.

Aaron Davis Cohen (1865–1889)

A Jewish tailor who was found wandering about the streets of Whitechapel, Cohen was arrested for vagrancy after the killings and sent to a workhouse infirmary. An actual raving lunatic, he became upon incarceration violent and dangerous, according to the doctors, having to be restrained and segregated from the other inmates.

The only contention that Cohen was the Ripper was made by an author who states that he thought Cohen was in fact a suspect named by Sir Robert Anderson.

Cohen died in a weakened condition in an asylum at the end of 1889.

Dr. Morgan Davies (1854–1920)

A native of Whitechapel and doctor at London Hospital, Dr. Davies was suspected of being the Ripper by R. D. Stephenson. Stephenson became convinced of this after he had supposedly witnessed a performance wherein Davies imitated the Ripper, and this was so realistic to Stephenson that he thought Davies must certainly be the lunatic that everyone was looking for.

Together with an ironmonger named George Marsh, Stephenson began to spy on Davies, eventually going to Scotland Yard with his suspicions. The police apparently took what he told them with a grain of salt.

Henry James

Railway signalman Thomas Ede testified at the Nichols inquest that he had seen a suspicious-looking man with a sharp-looking knife sticking out of his pocket shortly after the second Ripper murder. The man had a wooden arm, and behaved in a peculiar manner.

Five days after his original testimony, Ede returned to state that he had discovered that the man was none other than Henry James, a harmless lunatic living in the East End district.

Joseph Isaacs

A cigar maker and petty thief, Joseph Isaacs was suspected of being the Ripper by a lodging house keeper. Isaacs was known to pace his room at night, and this seemed suspicious enough to arouse the lodging house keeper.

Isaacs finally did something really odd—he moved out of the house the day after the Mary Kelly murder. Police were called and put Isaacs under observation when he returned to the lodging house to recover a violin bow that he had left there. He was then arrested for stealing a watch from a pawnbroker. Inspector Abberline took him under guard to the police station, and the press erroneously assumed that the Ripper had been captured.

George Gissing (1857–1903)

A very thin case has been presented against George Gissing, a noted author of the late nineteenth century and who also lectured at a university.

He was forced to leave his post after marrying a prostitute, and some researchers, although few, see a parallel with certain details in his writings, suggesting that he was the Ripper. This is unlikely in the extreme.

Vassilly Konovalov

Another Russian, possibly confused with Michael Ostrog, there were no fewer than three men of this name who have been traced as living in 1888.

The theory here is much the same as with Ostrog: Konovalov was an agent of Ochrana, the Russian secret police, sent to London to perform the murders in order to discredit the English police. He also allegedly was wanted in connection with the murder of a woman in Paris in 1887.

Nicholas Vassilly (b. 1842)

Press reports of 1888 alleged that Vassilly, a Russian by birth, had emigrated to France where he killed five prostitutes after failing to reform them (or at least killed one with whom he was supposed to have lived). He was supposedly released from the asylum in France where he had been incarcerated, at the beginning of 1888, went to the East End of London, and murdered five more prostitutes.

Charles Ludwig (b. 1848)

Ludwig was a German-born hairdresser who settled in the White-chapel area. After the first two Ripper murders, Ludwig accosted a prostitute and threatened her with a knife. Ludwig escaped when she called a policeman.

A few hours later, Ludwig threatened a customer at a coffee stall with a knife. This time he was caught and arrested. It was discovered that Ludwig had a bad temper and had threatened other people with knives and razors. Ludwig was still in jail when the murders of Elizabeth Stride and Catherine Eddowes were committed, and thus was not Jack the Ripper.

Jose Laurenco (b. 1862)

A Portuguese sailor on a cattle boat that docked in England, Laurenco was suspected by theorists of the late nineteenth century, who believed that he may have committed one, or possibly more, of the murders.

Edward Larkins, a customs clerk, believed Laurenco acted in association with several other Portuguese seamen. He passed on his suspicions to the police, who determined that Larkins was a crank.

James Kelly (d. 1929)

Claimed by a recent author to be Jack the Ripper, Kelly did in fact commit one murder for certain—that was of his wife in 1883.

Kelly had his death sentence commuted to life imprisonment in Broadmoor, from which he escaped in early 1888. He was in America about eight years later, then went back to England where he turned himself in at Broadmoor in 1927, after nearly forty years of freedom.

The only reason I include Kelly here is that author John Morrison assures us he has documented proof that Kelly is the Ripper, but all we have so far is Morrison's word for it.

Dr. John Hewitt (1850–1892)

A Manchester doctor and former veterinary student, Hewitt was placed in a lunatic asylum sometime prior to the murders. He was in the asylum in 1888, but during the Ripper scare he was allowed out on his own several times. It would seem, however, that Hewitt was in the asylum, Coton Hill, on the specific murder dates.

William Henry Bury (1859–1889)

Scottish murderer who, two months before he was executed, was written up in the *New York Times* as Jack the Ripper. The evidence for this consisted of the words someone had chalked on a door at Bury's flat: "Jack the Ripper is at the back of this door," and "Jack the Ripper is in this sellar [*sic*]."

The *Times* concluded that Mrs. Bury, who was strangled and then abdominally mutilated, had discovered her husband's true identity, so he had to silence her. Scottish author Euan MacPherson tends to agree with this theory.

Edward Buchan (1859–1888)

Author Roger Barber names Edward Buchan as his choice for Jack the Ripper. The only evidence to support this, if one can actually refer to it that way, is that Buchan, a shoemaker from Poplar, committed suicide ten days following the murder of Mary Kelly in Miller's Court. Barber reasons that Buchan died and the murders ceased; ergo, Buchan must have been the Ripper.

George Hutchinson

George Hutchinson, not to be confused with the witness of the same name in the Mary Kelly murder, was written up in the *Pall Mall Gazette* in early 1889 as a possible Jack the Ripper candidate.

Apparently he was handy with a knife, carving little figures out of animal bones that he had obtained from a slaughterhouse, and had mutilated a woman in Chicago in a similar fashion as the Ripper victims. He had escaped from a lunatic asylum around 1885 and had not been seen since.

4. POLITICIANS AND POLICE

This chapter deals with all the relevant people running the country who were directly (or very infrequently indirectly) involved in some aspect of the Whitechapel crimes.

As for politicians (Queen Victoria is included as well), their roles were primarily as liaisons to the police, although allegations of a conspiracy among these prestigious people has also been proposed and will be discussed.

The police involved in the case are numerous, and I apologize if I have left anyone out. It is difficult to list everyone who was involved; I have included those police who were at the scene of a murder, saw the victims either alive or dead, or gave evidence at their inquests. Some did all three.

All the well-known as well as some previously unknown or obscure members of the police will be discussed in this chapter. I begin with those of higher rank, graduating down to the lower echelon.

POLITICIANS

Queen Victoria (1819–1901)

The reigning monarch of the British Empire from 1837 until her death sixty-four years later, Queen Victoria went into deep mourning following the death of her husband, Prince Albert, in 1868. It was not so deep, however, that she paid no attention to or was unaware of the goings-on around her.

Victoria was very sensitive to and concerned about the Jack the Ripper crimes. Henrietta Barnett, wife of the well-known social reformer Reverend Samuel Barnett, sent the queen a petition she had drafted on behalf of the women of the East End with more than four thousand signatures affixed.

Victoria expressed concern over the poor conditions in the East End district, especially the lighting (or lack of it) and was shrewd enough to note that all the murders were committed on weekends. This led her to suggest to the police that all cattle boats and passenger ships should be searched. (Shipping registers show that cattle boats and other such vessels habitually docked on weekends. During the week they were working on the rivers. Their crews, then, would be in town on weekends.) She also suggested that single men living alone should be investigated, and finally that more policemen should be assigned to the Whitechapel area.

Robert Gascoyne Cecil, Marquess of Salisbury (1830–1903)

The prime minister of England during the reign of terror of Jack the Ripper, Lord Salisbury has been proposed by some theorists to have been the triggering mechanism of the Freemasonry conspiracy, which was allegedly carried out by Sir William Gull and others. Lord Salisbury, by the way, was not a Freemason.

On 10 November 1888, the day after Mary Kelly was murdered in Miller's Court, Salisbury was upbraided in a telegram from the queen in which she reminded him of a promise he had made to see to it that the lighting in Whitechapel would be upgraded.

That very same afternoon, Salisbury issued a statement from 10 Downing Street: "At Cabinet today it was resolved to issue a Proclamation offering free pardon to anyone who should give evidence as to the recent murders, except the actual perpetrator of the crimes."

Lord Henry Matthews (1826–1913)

The home secretary during the Ripper murders, Henry Matthews came under criticism by politicians of all parties (as well as the press) for provoking the resignations of both Metropolitan Police Commissioner Sir Charles Warren and James Monro, C.I.D.

A hostile press and public alike cried for Matthews's resignation at the time of the killings, but Lord Salisbury was afraid that his government would fall if Matthews resigned; Salisbury refused to allow him.

Matthews caused friction among just about everyone in the government. He was wishy-washy in attitude, and this lack of decisiveness tended to exacerbate problems that he faced. He was sensitive to criticism and was thought to be unable to get along or interact in a productive or positive manner with those whom he needed to deal with.

Matthews received harsh criticism from all quarters for his refusal to offer a reward in connection with the Whitechapel murders, although that decision was not his alone.

Godfrey Lushington (1832–1907)

Lawyer and permanent under secretary during the significant period, Godfrey Lushington acted as a liaison between Home Secretary Henry Matthews and Sir Charles Warren. At least this was what he was supposed to be doing. According to Sir Robert Anderson, however, Lushington was actually to blame for the ill will that existed between the two men, and also exacerbated problems among James Monro, Warren, and Matthews.

POLICE

Sir Charles Warren (1840–1927)

The Metropolitan Police commissioner, 1886–1888, Sir Charles Warren had already had a distinguished career in a number of areas. He was an engineer, soldier, author, and one of the most high-ranking Freemasons in the world; he had founded a number of Masonic Lodges and had others named for him.

In his army career he was the general who relieved his good friend General Gordon at Khartoum, and after he resigned from the Met, he returned to the army where he served with distinction in the Boer War. He later assisted General Lord Robert Baden-Powell with the Boy Scouts.

In 1886, then home secretary Hugh Childers appointed Warren commissioner of the Metropolitan Police. This was a move popular with everyone; the press was quick to support Warren's appointment, but two years later they would turn on him. Unfortunately, Warren soon made a few mistakes, which were blown out of proportion by the press (especially the radical press), and not helped by the new home secretary, Henry Matthews.

Certain members of the press continued to attack Warren for the remainder of his tenure following a riot that occurred on Sunday, 13 November 1887 in Trafalgar Square. Warren was quite correct to call in mounted troops to control the crowd, which had become ugly and eventually got out of hand. Many were injured, but only one person died. Meanwhile, Matthews was busy stirring up trouble between Warren and his eventual successor, James Monro. Monro had broken off from the C.I.D. and created his own department.

Warren was severely criticized by the press during his involvement in the Jack the Ripper murders. Most of this "bad press" was due to the radical element, who had still not let up on Warren since "Bloody Sunday" the previous year.

Warren did two things at least that are worth mentioning for their relevance to this period. The first was an act of stupidity on Warren's part. Following the double murder of Stride and Eddowes on 30 September, Police Constable Alfred Long discovered a piece of bloody apron, later proven to have belonged to Eddowes, in Goulston Street. Directly above the apron on a wall was a chalked message that read, "The Juwes are the men that will not be blamed for nothing."

The apron was definitely a clue, the only tangible one the Ripper ever left, and the message had not been on the wall thirty minutes before Long discovered it, as another policeman had walked his beat and seen that the wall was clean.

Superintendent Thomas Arnold arrived at the scene and was anxious to have the writing erased. He (as well as Warren) felt that the message was anti-Semitic in nature and might be a cause of riots. Warren ordered its removal; in fact some sources claim that Warren actually erased it personally. Sir Henry Smith testified that he had been informed of Warren's erasure of the message when Coroner Samuel Langham asked him about it during the Eddowes inquest.

There is no doubt that Warren was responsible for the removal of the message, which could have easily been partitioned off and guarded until photographers arrived. Sir Henry Smith and Superintendent McWilliam both wanted the message photographed.

Many helpful suggestions to trap the killer had been put forward in the newspapers, and in October Edwin Brough of Scarborough wrote to suggest the use of bloodhounds. Brough, a champion breeder of bloodhounds, offered the services of two of his prized hounds, Burgho and Barnaby, which he put at the disposal of the police. Evidently Warren liked this idea and had Brough bring the dogs to London. Early on a foggy morning, Warren agreed to be the "bait" for the dogs to hunt; all went well at first, but then the dogs lost Warren, and eventually became lost themselves on Tooting Common. The police had to send out a search party to track the dogs. The press pilloried Warren over this episode.

The next month Warren gave an unauthorized press interview in which he told of the problems he was having getting things done. Warren finally resigned a few hours before the Mary Kelly murder in Miller's Court on 9 November. Although he had already formally resigned, police officers at the scene were unaware of this, waiting for Warren to arrive with the bloodhounds, who were also unavailable.

Sir Henry Smith (1835–1921)

The popular acting commissioner during the absence of Sir James Fraser at the time of the Whitechapel murders, Smith controlled the City of London Police, and when Catherine Eddowes was murdered in Mitre Square on 30 September, it came under Smith's jurisdiction.

Smith had been on the alert, sleeping at Cloak Lane Police Station, when he was awakened in the small hours of the morning and informed of the murder. Smith jumped into a cab and was whisked off to Mitre Square.

Smith testified before Coroner Samuel Langham at the Eddowes inquest that he had been told that Sir Charles Warren had personally erased the chalked message in Goulston Street. This made Smith indignant, and rightly so, as it was an act of stupidity. The press seemed to feel that Smith and the City Police would be more apt to catch Jack the Ripper than their Metropolitan counterparts under Sir Charles Warren.

Smith took an active part in the investigation, and the newspapers seemed happy with his cooperation with them. In writing his memoirs, Smith said that he probably knew more about the murders than any other member of the police, including Sir Robert Anderson, in whom Smith had little faith. This statement not only rankled certain contemporaries of Smith, but has also been questioned by authors and researchers.

Sir Robert Anderson (1841–1918)

Irish-born Anderson began his career as a lawyer, later becoming an intelligence official whose specialty was dealing with spies and political crimes, notably Irish terrorism.

Just before the Whitechapel murders began, Anderson was appointed to replace James Monro as assistant commissioner of the C.I.D. There was naturally some infighting among the higher echelon of the police, but generally speaking, Anderson's colleagues praised him.

Brimming with confidence, Anderson left for Switzerland on holiday on 8 September 1888. He thought that the Nichols murder would be easily solved and did not attach particular importance to it. He was not to know that this murder would be just one in a series of horrible crimes.

The very same day that Anderson left England, Annie Chapman was killed, and by the time he returned in early October, Elizabeth Stride and Catherine Eddowes had also been slain.

The vacillating Henry Matthews, home secretary, and Sir Charles Warren felt that Anderson should have been in the country (or possibly have returned back sooner), but he was not to know of events to come.

Anderson proposed several measures, one of which was adopted: prostitutes would not be able to count on protection from the police—which is not to say that they ever had. Anderson remained in close contact with James Monro and Chief Superintendent Donald Swanson throughout the remainder of the Ripper scare.

Much has been made of Anderson's statements after the crimes—both in his autobiography and elsewhere—that the police knew the identity of the Ripper. While not actually naming him, Anderson says that he was a Polish Jew living in the Whitechapel district. He said that the suspect's people "would not give him up" to justice, and further claimed that the only reliable witness, who was also Jewish, refused to testify against him, although he had unhesitatingly identified him.

Anderson gave as his reasons for not revealing the man's identity the beliefs that, first, it would not show the police force in a very good light and, second, it would not be in the best interests of the public.

James Monro (1838–1920)

James Monro was relieved of his job as assistant Metropolitan Police commissioner and replaced by Sir Robert Anderson just before the Jack the Ripper murders began. With the resignation of Sir Charles Warren on 8 November 1888, Monro was made Metropolitan Police commissioner.

In between (in other words, during the ten and a half weeks of the murders), Monro headed a special detective service that had been created specifically for him, and liaised with the Metropolitan Police. At this time Monro was given "unofficial" status.

Monro was a man of pride who resigned several posts during his career rather than be told what to do. He felt that if he was put in charge, he should be able to make his own decisions. A detective highly respected by those who worked with him, Monro did nevertheless get under the skin of several of his colleagues, most notably Sir Charles Warren, over what seems in retrospect nothing more than a series of petty departmental squabbles.

Many members of the press felt that Monro should have been put in charge of the Ripper case, as his past record indicated that he was intelligent as well as popular with his men, especially after putting in much time and hard work on his pension proposal for policemen.

Years after the murders, Monro made a cryptic comment to a
member of his family: "Jack the Ripper was never caught, but he
should have been." There has been much speculation as to
exactly what he meant by the remark. Unfortunately he did not
expound on it.

Sir Melville MacNaghten (1853–1921)

Sir Melville Leslie MacNaghten became assistant chief constable
of the C.I.D. the year following the Ripper murders, and is
noteworthy for (among other things) making the remark, "The
greatest regret of my lifetime was that I joined the force six
months after Jack the Ripper committed suicide."

MacNaghten's contribution to the Ripper affair consists of a
memorandum that he penned in 1894 which included some
interesting comments. First, MacNaghten indicates Montague J.
Druitt as Jack the Ripper, stating that in all probability the Ripper
had put an end to himself after his brain finally gave way
following the Mary Kelly murder, and certain facts came to light
several years after the crimes. These facts were supposedly
unknown to the police in 1888.

He further stated that the Whitechapel murderer killed five
victims and five victims only (Mary Ann Nichols, Annie
Chapman, Elizabeth Stride, Catherine Eddowes, and Mary Kelly).

MacNaghten writes that although there were many suspects at
the time, including a number of lunatics wandering about the East
End, the police had very strong suspicions against three men in
particular. They were:

> 1: Mr. M. J. Druitt, a doctor [Druitt was a lawyer] of about 41
> years of age (Druitt's actual age was 31 at the time) and of
> fairly good family, who disappeared at the time of the Miller's
> Court murder, and whose body was found floating in the
> Thames on 31st December, i.e. seven weeks after the said
> murder. The body was said to have been in the water a month
> or more—on it was found a season ticket to Blackheath and
> London. He was sexually insane and from private information
> I have little doubt that his own family suspected this man of
> being the Whitechapel murderer.

2: [Aaron] Kosminski, a Polish Jew who lived in the very heart of the Whitechapel district where the murders were committed. He had become insane owing to many years of solitary vices. He had a great hatred of women, with strong homicidal tendencies. He was (and I believe still is) detained in a lunatic asylum about March 1889. This man in appearance strongly resembled the individual seen by the city P.C. near Mitre Square. There were many circs. connected with this man which made him a strong suspect.

3: Michael Ostrog, a mad Russian doctor and convict and unquestionably a homicidal maniac. This man is said to have been habitually cruel to women, and for a long time was known to have carried about with him surgical knives and other instruments; his antecedents were of the very worst possible type, and his whereabouts at the time of the Whitechapel murders could never be satisfactorily accounted for. He is still alive.

Regarding the aforementioned, MacNaghten wrote: "Personally after much careful and deliberate consideration, I am inclined to exonerate the last two, but I have always held strong opinions regarding number one, and the more I think the matter over, the stronger do these opinions become."

Colonel Sir James Fraser (1814–1892)

The commissioner of the City of London Police, seventy-four-year-old Sir James Fraser, a former soldier, was on leave when Catherine Eddowes was murdered in Mitre Square on 30 September. This territory—the square mile of the City of London—fell within the boundaries of Fraser's command. In his absence Sir Henry Smith took charge of the case, and on his return Fraser was content to let Smith continue to handle the matter.

Fraser, who always got along well with everyone (one of the very rare people in the whole affair who did), suggested to the lord mayor of London that a reward of £ 500 be offered to anyone who could help apprehend the killer. This suggestion was well received, and the reward was offered in the name of the Corporation of the City of London.

Chief Constable Frederick P. Wensley (1865–1949)

Wensley at the time of the Whitechapel murders was a humble constable who, along with scores of others, patrolled the streets of the East End. He commented later that the strips of rubber nailed to the standard police boot were the forerunner of rubber-soled boots.

Wensley is notable because he is the first ordinary man to rise through the ranks of constable to the higher echelons of the police.

Wensley retired after a brilliant forty-year career; his great successes came after the Ripper murders. His autobiography, published in 1931, provides a valuable picture of the police force and the Ripper investigation as seen through the eyes of a twenty-three-year-old constable.

Chief Constable Bolton Monsell

Generally acting as a liaison between the commissioners and other ranks of the police force, Monsell's part in the Ripper affair consisted mainly of providing written and oral reports.

Monsell was called to the scene of the Nichols murder in Buck's Row after her body had been removed to the mortuary in Old Montague Street. He was also at the scene in the backyard of 29 Hanbury Street on 8 September, where Annie Chapman was killed.

Chief Constable Frederick Williamson (1830–1889)

A man who rose very quickly up the ladder in the police force, Williamson was the C.I.D.'s senior policeman during the Whitechapel murders.

Williamson was a very sick man at this time, and his exact contributions to the investigation were naturally minimal. He was succeeded the following year, when he died, by Sir Melville MacNaghten, who had been James Monro's original choice for the post.

Superintendent Thomas Arnold (b. 1835)

A former soldier and head of H Division, Whitechapel, at the time of the crimes, Arnold had just returned from leave when the double murders of Stride and Eddowes occurred on 30 September. Arnold was particularly interested in having the chalked message erased from the wall in Goulston Street, much to his discredit.

Some time after 1:00 P.M. on the afternoon of 9 November 1888, Arnold arrived in Miller's Court, where Mary Kelly's mutilated corpse had been discovered by Thomas Bowyer, who had gone there to collect the rent. That was 10:45 A.M.

Inspector Walter Beck was the first police officer to arrive at the scene, and was followed by Inspector Frederick Abberline, who got to Miller's Court about 11:30. They did not enter the room until Arnold arrived, informing them of Sir Charles Warren's resignation and giving the order for landlord John McCarthy to break open the door.

Arnold affixed his signature to the statement made by George Hutchinson at the police station on 12 November.

Chief Inspector Donald Swanson (1848–1924)

Scottish-born Donald Swanson was put in charge of the murder investigation right from the beginning, the day after the murder of Mary Ann Nichols in Buck's Row. Swanson was replaced by Sir Robert Anderson, a personal friend, at the beginning of October. It was in Swanson's copy of the Anderson autobiography, *My Official Life,* that Swanson penciled in specific comments under details of the Ripper case. Swanson's grandson had these notes published in a newspaper more than seventy years afterward.

Swanson wrote that Kosminski was the unnamed Anderson suspect. Swanson also wrote that following Kosminski's identification, there were no more Ripper murders committed. Swanson made these notes more than twenty years after the murders.

Chief Inspector West

With the temporary absence of Superintendent Thomas Arnold, who was on leave, West was made acting superintendent during the murders of Mary Ann Nichols and Annie Chapman.

Not much is known about this man, but he did write a memorandum to Scotland Yard concerning the Ripper case. West stated in reference to Annie Chapman's murder at 29 Hanbury Street that he felt that Inspector Abberline should be put in charge of the case, as West knew that Abberline was already handling the Mary Ann Nichols investigation, and from the evidence it seemed conclusive that both murders had been committed by the same person.

Chief Inspector Henry Moore (b. 1848)

Moore acted as a liaison between Inspector Frederick Abberline, who was in charge of all police in the field, and desk officer Chief Inspector Donald Swanson during the Ripper investigation.

A year following the end of the killings, Moore gave a newspaper interview in which he described the horrible scene in Miller's Court where Mary Jane Kelly's mutilated remains were found.

Chief Inspector James Stockley (1863–1954)

James Stockley's greatest successes occurred after the Ripper case, as he was only twenty-five years old at the time of the killings.

Stockley adopted a variety of disguises in the Whitechapel district at the time of the murders, hoping to catch the Ripper.

Inspector Frederick Abberline (1843–1929)

The year before the Jack the Ripper murders, Inspector Frederick Abberline had already had twenty-five years of distinguished police service behind him when James Monro requested his transfer to Scotland Yard.

Abberline was in charge of all detectives in the field at the time of the Ripper inquiries. He had been an inspector in the White-chapel district (H Division) for fifteen years by 1888. Abberline was a hardworking and highly respected policeman who received numerous awards for his excellence throughout a distinguished career that spanned some thirty years.

In published interviews fifteen years after the murders, Abberline stated that he always thought that George Chapman was Jack the Ripper. When Chapman was arrested for a series of poisonings in 1892, Abberline supposedly remarked to arresting officer George Godley, ''You've got Jack the Ripper at last.''

Abberline's reasons for selecting Chapman as the Ripper are weak—they included the point that after Chapman left England for America some time following the killings, there were no more. By the same token, Abberline states that Montague J. Druitt's suicide at the end of the year does not mean anything—just a coincidence. Abberline further states in the interview that the police of 1888 did not know the identity of the Ripper, a statement that is a direct contradiction to statements made by several other high-ranking police officials.

Inspector John Spratling (1840–1935)

The divisional inspector of J Division, John Spratling was called in at the first murder, that of Mary Ann Nichols, in Buck's Row on 31 August 1888. He arrived at the scene at 4:30 A.M.

By that time, Spratling testified to Wynne Baxter at the inquest, Dr. Rees R. Llewelyn had already arrived to make his examination of the body, and Nichols had been removed to the mortuary shed at the Workhouse Infirmary in Old Montague Street. James Green was washing the blood from the street.

Spratling then went to the mortuary in order to take down a description of the body, and while there he discovered that Nichols had been disemboweled. Spratling then sent someone to fetch Dr. Llewelyn so that he could make a more detailed examination.

Spratling personally and immediately searched the murder area and other nearby points in the East End with Detective Sergeant George Godley, but the two men found nothing of interest.

Spratling's report regarding the injuries to Nichols ran as follows:

> Her throat had been cut from left to right, two distinct cuts being on the left side, the windpipe, gullet, and spinal cord being cut through, a bruise apparently of a thumb being on the right lower jaw, also one on the left cheek.

The abdomen had been cut open from centre of bottom ribs, on the right side and under pelvis to the left of the stomach; there the wound was jagged.

The omentum, or coating of the stomach was also cut in several places and there were some small stabs on private parts, apparently done with a strong-bladed knife, supposed to have been done by some left-handed person, death almost instantaneous.

Inspector Joseph L. Chandler (b. 1850)

At 6:00 A.M. on 8 September, Chandler was fetched from Commercial Street Police Station to go to nearby Hanbury Street, where Annie Chapman's body had been discovered by John Davis, a resident of No. 29.

Chandler arrived on the scene a very few minutes after he had been notified, as Hanbury Street was just around the corner. He ordered the dispersal of the small crowd that had gathered, and took a verbal report from John Davis. He also ordered the body to be covered with sacking; James Kent fetched a canvas and covered it up.

Chandler sent for Dr. George B. Phillips, who arrived at 6:30 and made a preliminary examination of Chapman's body. At this time Chandler was searching the yard for any signs of evidence. He also organized a search of the neighboring yards and found nothing.

Several days later a bloodstained piece of paper was found in the Bayley's backyard at No. 23; Chandler stated that it had not been there when the yard was searched on the day of the murder. Chandler also determined that stains on the fence of the backyard of No. 25, which had been brought to the attention of the police by a little girl named Laura Sickings (who was a resident of No. 25), were urine and not bloodstains.

Inspector Joseph Henry Helson (b. 1845)

A C.I.D. inspector, Joseph Helson was involved in the White-chapel investigation from the onset. After Inspector Spratling had arrived at the mortuary and discovered the full extent of Mary

Ann Nichols's injuries, Helson arrived at some point later, where he found that the body had been washed by paupers James Hatfield and Robert Mann, apparently against Spratling's orders.

Helson itemized the possessions of the deceased, and attempted to ascertain her identity. He also testified at the inquest that he passed along this information to Scotland Yard.

Following the Chapman murder, Helson put out the all-points bulletin for John Pizer, known as "Leather Apron." Pizer was subsequently arrested by Sergeant William Thicke on 10 September. Helson also spoke to Inspector Frederick Abberline, telling him that he was certain that Mary Ann Nichols and Annie Chapman were murdered by the same person.

Inspector Walter Beck (b. 1852)

Inspector Walter Beck was involved in the Mary Kelly investigation. Following the discovery of the body by Thomas Bowyer, landlord John McCarthy went running to Commercial Road Police Station, where he found Beck. Beck arrived with McCarthy at Miller's Court at about 11:00 A.M., apparently the first policeman at the scene.

Half an hour later, Inspector Frederick Abberline arrived, and the two inspectors went into consultation. It became apparent that neither man knew of Sir Charles Warren's resignation, as they waited for his arrival. It was only after Superintendent Arnold arrived that it was learned Warren was not coming. Beck later testified at the Kelly inquest on 10 November.

Inspector Walter Andrews (b. 1847)

Walter Andrews was a Scotland Yard inspector who was sent to Whitechapel to work on the Ripper case. He worked closely with Inspector Abberline as well as with Chief Inspector Henry Moore.

Andrews, who was apparently well liked and admired by his men, went to America about six weeks after the Mary Kelly murder, acting on information that a suspect had left on a ship bound for New York. The press carried the headlines "Jack the Ripper in U.S.A."

Inspector Edmund Reid (b. 1846)

A most versatile and accomplished man, Reid had achieved high
standards as an actor, singer, and magician while still in his early
career with the police.

When James Monro asked for Inspector Frederick Abberline to
be moved over to Scotland Yard in 1887, Reid replaced him as
head of Whitechapel's H Division. Although Reid was involved
in the investigation, he apparently did not pay much attention to
details (or else suffered from a poor memory), as several years
after the killings he was quoted in the press as saying there were
nine Jack the Ripper murders, and no organs were missing from
the bodies of any of the victims. He also thought that the knife
used in the killings had been blunt.

Inspector Edward Collard (1846–1892)

Inspector Edward Collard was on duty in Bishopsgate Police
Station the early morning of 30 September 1888, when the double
murders of Elizabeth Stride and Catherine Eddowes took place.

Eddowes had been arrested for being drunk and disorderly
earlier in the evening by Police Constable Louis Robinson, and
brought to Bishopsgate, where she was eventually released from
custody at 1:00 A.M. by P.C. George Hutt.

Collard was informed of the murder and went immediately to
Mitre Square, arriving at the same time as City Police Surgeon Dr.
Frederick Gordon Brown. Collard organized a house-to-house
search of the neighborhood, and later testified before Coroner
S. F. Langham at the Eddowes inquest.

Inspector Charles Pinhorn (b. 1849)

Following Louis Diemschutz's discovery of the body of Elizabeth
Stride in Dutfield's Yard, Berner Street, at about one o'clock on
the morning of 30 September, Inspector Pinhorn was sent for.
Doctors Blackwell and Phillips had already arrived by the time

Pinhorn and Acting Superintendent West came to the site. Pinhorn immediately took control of the investigation at the scene.

Inspector James McWilliam

Chiefly acting as a liaison to Chief Inspector Donald Swanson, McWilliam was in charge of the City Police. This ties in directly with the Eddowes murder, which came under City Police jurisdiction.

McWilliam was angered over Sir Charles Warren's stupidity in having the chalked message erased in Goulston Street, as was Sir Henry Smith. Since the message was found in an area under Metropolitan Police authority, it was Warren's decision by right, even if it was the wrong thing to do.

A popular person with the newspapers, McWilliam was criticized by Home Secretary Henry Matthews for the report he had submitted regarding the Eddowes case. Matthews commented that the report was so long and labyrinthine that it was of little value.

Inspector James Cunningham (b. 1868)

Cunningham was new to the police force in 1888. His primary function during the Whitechapel horrors was patrolling the East End, sometimes in uniform and occasionally in plain clothes. His noteworthy success came after the crimes, and he enjoyed a long and distinguished career.

Inspector William Cansby (b. 1852)

Cansby became involved in the case following the Annie Chapman murder in Hanbury Street. He instructed Sergeant Thicke to arrest John Pizer, known as "Leather Apron," on 10 September.

Cansby then arranged a lineup in which Pizer was picked out by a witness; however, lacking other evidence, Cansby ordered Pizer's release on the following day.

Inspector Izzard

An inspector with the City of London Police, Izzard was called to Mitre Square following the discovery of the body of Catherine Eddowes. He was put in charge of restoring and maintaining order in the area and dispersing the curious crowd that gathered and got in the way. Sergeants Dudman and Phelps assisted him.

Inspector Richard Webb (b. 1851)

A former soldier, Webb had been made a divisional inspector with J Division the year prior to the murders.

Although his exact part in the investigation is not known, on Webb's retirement in 1899 the *Police Review* ran a feature on his career that said he took "a very active part" in the investigation. That part, however, is not defined.

Detective Superintendent Alfred Foster (1826–1897)

A former solicitor, Alfred Foster joined the City of London Police force at the behest of Sir James Fraser. When informed of the Eddowes murder, Foster went to Mitre Square and saw the body. He also questioned witnesses the day following the murder, but learned nothing to excite interest. Foster was a popular man with the press, as he did his best to keep them informed and was always a paragon of courtesy and frankness.

Detective Baxter Hunt

A former member of the Metropolitan Police, Baxter Hunt was with the City Police Force at the time Catherine Eddowes was murdered in Mitre Square.

Along with Detective Constable Daniel Halse, Hunt went from the square to examine the chalked message that Constable Alfred Long had discovered at the Wentworth Dwellings in Goulston Street. Hunt also played a key role in establishing the identity of the victim.

Detective Sergeant George Godley (1858–1941)

George Godley was very much involved in the Ripper investigation from the first murder to the last. Along with Inspector John Spratling, Godley searched railway yards, embankments, and lines in the East End immediately following the Mary Ann Nichols murder. Godley subsequently took notes at her inquest, which he observed on behalf of the C.I.D.

Godley was present in Miller's Court on 9 November when Mary Jane Kelly's body was discovered, arriving just moments after Inspector Walter Beck.

In 1892 Godley arrested George Chapman for a series of poisonings, and Inspector Frederick Abberline remarked to him, "You've got Jack the Ripper at last." Chapman never admitted to being the Ripper, and was subsequently hanged. Throughout the series of murders, Godley was quoted by the press, who found him a well-informed and cooperative man.

Detective Sergeant Patrick Enright (b. 1849)

Attached to Whitechapel's J Division, Detective Sergeant Patrick Enright went to the mortuary in Old Montague Street on the morning of 31 August. At the mortuary, Inspector Spratling had given specific orders that the body not be touched, which he passed on to Enright. The orders (if in fact they had been passed down the line) were, however, ignored by the paupers who laid out the body.

In company with several other members of the police, Enright witnessed the Nichols inquest, although he apparently did not give evidence. He later followed up a clue given by several independent witnesses, which may or may not have had something to do with "Leather Apron." This clue was probably not related to John Pizer, however, because Pizer had been released from custody on 11 September and the clue was reported in the newspapers on the twentieth of that month.

Detective Sergeant Robert Outram

Like a great many other City Police detectives, Robert Outram's career was primarily concerned with bank frauds and the like. He attained the rank of detective inspector by the time he retired.

Outram was nearby St. Bolton's Church, Houndsditch, when men came running up with the news of the Eddowes murder. He then went to Mitre Square about quarter past two in the morning as a reinforcement, in company with two other policemen.

Detective Constable Robert Sagar (1852–1924)

A former medical student, Sagar gave up that career to become a policeman, and Sir Henry Smith gave Sagar high praise at the conclusion of his twenty-five-year career.

Sagar stated in his memoirs that the police had strong suspicions of a certain man who lived in Aldgate, and who Sagar was certain was insane. According to Sagar, the man's family apparently had him removed to an asylum, where he died. Sagar does not name the man. A newspaper obituary said that Sagar "played a leading part" in the investigation.

Detective Constable Walter Dew (1863–1947)

Walter Dew, a detective constable in Whitechapel's H Division, is probably most famous as the man who caught Dr. Hawley Harvey Crippen (American-born British doctor who, along with his mistress, was charged with the murder of his wife [whose remains were buried and found in his coal cellar]. Crippen was hanged, while his mistress was acquitted.) He eventually attained the rank of chief inspector, and by his retirement from the police he had served nearly thirty years, afterward becoming a private detective.

In his memoirs, Dew is critical of the police's policy at the time of the Ripper investigation of giving too little information to the newspapers, which he felt contributed to a great deal of speculative reporting and creative journalism. Dew also comments on the procedures the police adopted in making arrests and questioning suspects. He personally did much legwork during the murders, and was one of the first police officers at the scene in Miller's Court—a horrifying memory which remained with Dew for the rest of his life.

Detective Constable Daniel Halse (b. 1839)

Daniel Halse gave vital testimony at the inquest of Catherine Eddowes before Coroner Samule F. Langham. In the company of detective constables Robert Outram and Edward Marriott, Halse was walking his beat in Houndsditch when men came running down the street with news of the murder at 2:00 A.M.

Halse testified that he heard watchman George Morris blowing his whistle from the direction of Mitre Square. His important evidence then went on: He had passed through Goulston Street about twenty minutes later—right next to where the chalked message and bloodied bit of apron were found half an hour later by P.C. Alfred Long. Neither was there when Halse went by. After learning of the existence of the apron and the message, Halse returned with Baxter Hunt to Goulston Street, where he (as well as Sir Henry Smith and Inspector McWilliam) urged that the message be photographed. Sir Charles Warren stupidly had it rubbed out.

Detective Constable Edward Marriott

Marriott was patrolling the streets near Houndsditch with Detective Constable Daniel Halse and Detective Sergeant Robert Outram in the small hours of 30 September 1888. Shortly after 2:00 A.M., Marriott and his fellow officers heard the tooting whistle of George Morris and arrived at Mitre Square, where Catherine Eddowes's mutilated remains had been discovered by P.C. Edward Watkins a short time before.

Sergeant William Thicke (1845–1930)

Prominently involved in the Whitechapel investigations, William Thicke is probably best remembered as the man who arrested boot-finisher John Pizer following the ''Leather Apron'' scare. John Richardson's soaking leather apron was found at the scene of Annie Chapman's murder at No. 29 Hanbury Street. Acting on orders from Inspector William Cansby, Thicke went to Pizer's residence at 22 Mulberry Street on the morning of 10 September, two days after the Chapman murder, and arrested Pizer.

A man of conspicuous appearance and superior knowledge of the Whitechapel-Spitalfields area, Thicke testified at the Chapman inquest on 13 September that he had known Pizer for nearly twenty years, and that he believed Pizer to be the "Leather Apron" they were seeking. He knew that Pizer habitually carried sharp knives on his person.

Thicke had been present when Emmanuel Violenia had picked Pizer out of a lineup, but after further questioning, Pizer was released.

Sergeant Stephen White (1854–1919)

White arrived in Berner Street shortly after the body of Elizabeth Stride had been discovered in Dutfield's Yard by Louis Diemschutz. On instructions from Chief Inspector Henry Moore, White's function at this time was to conduct a house-to-house search of the area and question everyone who lived nearby. In the course of these duties he interviewed fruiterer Matthew Packer. It was later ascertained by the two private detectives, Grand and Batchelor, that Packer had sold some black grapes to a man who was with Stride some time around midnight. White was sent again to question Packer, but the latter had by this time told all he knew in an official statement personally taken down by Sir Charles Warren.

In White's obituary, a story appeared that on the night of a murder (it does not specify which one), White supposedly met a man with brilliant eyes who seemed somehow odd to White, although he could not exactly pinpoint what about the man aroused his suspicions, and he had no legitimate reason to detain the man. Shortly after White's encounter with this man, a murder was discovered nearby. White was convinced that the man was Jack the Ripper. The obituary allegedly quotes from a report made by White when he was in disguise in the East End.

Sergeant Benjamin C. Leeson (b. 1870)

Leeson was not directly involved at the time in the Jack the Ripper murders as he did not join the police force until two and a half years after the final murder (that of Mary Kelly, 9 November). Leeson later wrote several articles, however, when he was in Australia. The articles in part described the general attitude of the police toward suspects at the time of the murders. Leeson points out that the murders were committed by someone skilled with a knife. He also states that during the murder period the police had under observation a certain doctor, who was supposedly always near at hand to the place the killings occurred, but Leeson does not name the doctor.

Sergeant Kerby

Sergeant Kerby was informed of the Mary Ann Nichols murder and was sent to Buck's Row on 31 August. He arrived shortly after 4:00 A.M. Dr. Ralph Llewelyn had arrived a few minutes before. With assistance from Police Constable John Thain, Kerby loaded Nichols's body onto a wagon and took it to the mortuary in Old Montague Street where Inspector Spratling eventually found the previously undiscovered injuries.

Sergeant Jones

Sergeant Jones arrived some time after Catherine Eddowes was found slain in Mitre Square. On the orders of an inspector, Jones searched the square with his lantern and found some interesting items: a thimble, three buttons apparently belonging to the victim, and a mustard tin containing pawn tickets that later helped to identify Eddowes. The pawnbroker's name happened to be Jones, too.

Sergeant James G. Byfield

James Byfield was the duty sergeant at Bishopsgate Police Station on the evening of 29 September, when P.C. Louis Robinson brought Catherine Eddowes in on a charge of drunk and disorderly conduct. Byfield locked her in a cell around 8:45 P.M. She was subsequently released at approximately 1:00 A.M. the following day.

Sergeant Barry

Sergeant Barry went with Sergeant William Thicke to the mortuary, transporting the body of Annie Chapman following her murder at 29

Hanbury Street. Barry wrote down Thicke's oral description of the body, which was identified later that morning by Amelia Palmer.

Sergeants Dudman and Phelps

These two sergeants, attached to the City of London Police, arrived in Mitre Square in the small hours of 30 September. Their job was to keep the peace and disperse the curious; they acted under the direct orders of Inspector Izzard.

Police Constable Alfred Long

P.C. Alfred Long made a very important discovery at the Wentworth Dwellings in Goulston Street immediately following the double murder of Elizabeth Stride and Catherine Eddowes on 30 September 1888. At about five or ten minutes prior to 3:00 A.M., Long, a member of the Metropolitan Police, noticed a bloody piece of apron lying on the pavement; it was subsequently identified as a piece of the apron that Catherine Eddowes had been wearing when she was murdered in Mitre Square. Just above the apron, chalked on the side wall of the building, was a message which read, "The Juwes are the men that will not be blamed for nothing."

Long notified his superiors and later testified at the inquest that the message and apron were not present when he had gone by the same spot half an hour previously. This was corroborated when Detective Constable Daniel Halse also stated that he had passed by the spot at about the time as Long did (2:20 A.M.) and the apron and message were not there. This would seem to be a definite clue left by the Ripper that indicated the direction he traveled after the Eddowes murder. Unfortunately, due to the stupidity of Sir Charles Warren, the message was obliterated before it could be photographed.

Police Constable Edward Watkins

On 30 September, Watkins was patrolling his beat and passed through Mitre Square at 1:30 A.M. At about this same time, Joseph

Lawende, Joseph Levy, and Harry Harris observed Catherine Eddowes (as she was later identified) talking to a man at the entrance to the square.

Constable James Harvey went by from the opposite direction to Watkins's beat on his own, which took him past the square at about 1:40 A.M. He neither saw nor heard anything untoward. Watkins returned to the square five minutes later and discovered Eddowes's disemboweled corpse. He proceeded to nearby Kearley & Tonge's Warehouse, where George Morris was night watchman. Morris, a former policeman, was familiar to Watkins. Watkins found Morris and said, "For God's sake, come to assist me; there's another woman cut up to pieces." Watkins could not understand how the murder had been committed in the short time since he had previously passed through the square.

Morris returned to Mitre Square with Watkins, then ran off blowing his whistle until help arrived. Watkins later testified at the Eddowes inquest, describing what he had seen: "She was ripped up like a pig in the market, her entrails flung in a heap about her neck."

Police Constable John Neil (b. 1850)

At about 3:40 A.M., 31 August 1888, carmen Charles Cross and John Paul discovered the body of Mary Ann Nichols in Buck's Row. Initially Cross thought the body was a tarpaulin, and Paul believed she was drunk; when they ascertained that her throat was cut and she was dead, they went to fetch a policeman.

Five minutes later, Police Constable John Neil came along on his beat and found the body. He saw another constable, P.C. John Thain, who was patrolling a short distance away, and discreetly signaled him with his lamp.

P.C. Jonas Mizen then approached from the opposite direction; Cross and Paul had told him about the murder and where to go. Police procedure at that time called for Neil, as the first policeman at the scene, to remain with the body. He sent Mizen to fetch an ambulance and Thain to get a doctor.

Thain returned first with Dr. Rees Ralph Llewelyn, who pronounced Nichols dead. By this time, three slaughtermen (Henry Tomkins, James Mumford, and Charles Brittain) had appeared and remained with Neil for a while.

After Llewelyn's brief examination, Sergeant Kerby arrived with the ambulance Mizen had instructed him to bring. Thain helped Kerby load the body, which was taken to the Old Montague Street mortuary.

Neil remained until Inspector John Spratling got to Buck's Row at 4:30 A.M., then went with the Inspector to the mortuary, where Spratling discovered the further injuries.

Police Constable Henry Lamb

Police Constable Henry Lamb was walking with Police Constable Edward Collins on their beats several hundred yards from Berner Street on the morning of 30 September.

Two members of the International Workingmen's Educational Club at 40 Berner Street—Morris Eagle and Isaac Kozebrodsky—notified them of the murder of Elizabeth Stride in Dutfield's Yard. Lamb sent Collins to fetch a doctor. Collins shortly returned to the scene with Dr. William P. Blackwell (at 1:15 A.M.). Forty-five minutes later, Dr. George Bagster Phillips arrived.

Lamb testified at the inquest, stating the he had sent two men to the police station for reinforcements, and he remained in Dutfield's Yard until after the body had been removed.

Police Constable Jonas Mizen (b. 1848)

Following the discovery of Mary Ann Nichols in Buck's Row, carmen Charles Cross and John Paul found Jonas Mizen in Hanbury Street just west of where they had discovered the body. Mizen arrived in Buck's Row to find police constables John Neil and John Thain already there. Neil had come across the body at 3:45 A.M.

Neil sent Mizen to fetch an ambulance and Thain to fetch a doctor. When Mizen returned with the ambulance, which was actually nothing more than a cart, Dr. Llewelyn had arrived and left. Sergeant Kerby then came along, removing the body in the ambulance Mizen had brought.

Police Constable Robert Spicer (b. 1866)

Twenty-two-year-old Robert Spicer was convinced that he had caught Jack the Ripper near Henage Court during the murder scare. Writing about the incident in 1931, Spicer observed that he saw a man in Henage Court talking to a prostitute whom he knew. The man carried a small black bag of American cloth and had blood on his shirt cuffs. Spicer described the man as neat in appearance, wearing a black suit, about 5 feet 8 inches tall, with a fair moustache and ruddy complexion.

Spicer arrested the man on suspicion of being Jack the Ripper, but upon taking him to the nearest police station the man identified himself as Dr. Frederick Chapman, a respectable Brixton doctor. Apparently this was enough to convince the police to let Chapman go, and Spicer could never understand that, although there were at least eight inspectors present, none of them made Chapman open his bag.

Police Constable John Thain

P.C. Thain was involved in the first murder, that of Mary Ann Nichols in Buck's Row on 31 August. He was called to the site at 3:45 A.M. by Police Constable John Neil, who had come across the body and signaled Thain with his lamp. Thain came up Buck's Row, and P.C. Jonas Mizen, who had been sent by carmen Charles Cross and John Paul, joined them from the opposite direction.

Neil then sent Thain to fetch Dr. Rees Ralph Llewelyn from his surgery at 152 Whitechapel Road. When Thain came back with the doctor, three local slaughtermen had also joined the group that was now forming near the body.

When Mizen brought back the ambulance, Thain helped Sergeant Kerby with the body, which Kerby took to the mortuary in Old Montague Street. Thain waited for the arrival of a senior police officer, and one came at 4:30 A.M. That was Inspector John Spratling.

Constable Thain testified before Wynne E. Baxter at the Nichols inquest.

Police Constable William Smith (b. 1862)

Constable William Smith saw Elizabeth Stride in the company of a man in Berner Street about half an hour before her body was discovered by jewelry salesman Louis Diemschutz. This may well have been the same man to whom Matthew Packer sold some black grapes around midnight.

Smith later identified Stride's body, and gave a description of the man as wearing dark-colored clothing, of medium build, about thirty years old, and 5 feet 7 inches tall.

Smith's beat took him again past the spot of the murder sometime after 1:00 A.M., when the body had already been discovered and several people were milling around. Smith then went for an ambulance.

Police Constable James Harvey

P.C. James Harvey passed right by the entrance to Mitre Square a mere five minutes before P.C. Edward Watkins discovered Catherine Eddowes's disemboweled body in the southwest corner of the square.

Harvey testified that although he did not actually enter the square itself, he heard and saw nothing near the entrance, Church Passage, which he passed through. Harvey's beat intersected that of Watkins at Mitre Square, the two men coming from opposite directions.

Police Constable Edward Collins

P.C. Edward Collins was on beat duty in Commercial Road with P.C. Henry Lamb on the morning of 30 September. Shortly after 1:00 A.M. two men—Morris Eagle and Isaac Kozebrodsky—ran up to tell them of the murder of Elizabeth Stride in Dutfield's Yard, Berner Street.

Collins went with Lamb and the two men back to the murder site, then went off to fetch a doctor, returning with Dr. William P. Blackwell at 1:15 A.M.

After Dr. Phillips arrived at 2:00 A.M. and also examined the body, Stride was eventually removed to the mortuary. Collins personally cleaned the bloodstains from the pavement.

Police Constable George Hutt

Hutt was on duty at Bishopsgate Police Station when P.C. Louis Robinson brought Catherine Eddowes in on a charge of drunken and disorderly conduct about 8:45 P.M. on 29 September.

At 12:30 A.M. on the thirtieth, Eddowes asked Hutt to release her. He did so about 1:00 or a few minutes before, telling her that it was too late for her to buy any more liquor. Eddowes told Hutt that she would receive "a damn fine hiding" when she returned home. "And it serves you right," Hutt replied. The last thing Eddowes said to Hutt on her way out the door was, "All right, good night, old cock," and she went off in the direction of Mitre Square.

Police Constable Louis F. Robinson

On the night of 29 September at 8:30 P.M., P.C. Robinson was patrolling in Aldgate when he came upon Catherine Eddowes rolling on the pavement imitating a fire engine. Eddowes was obviously the worse for drink, so with the assistance of Police Constable George Simmons, Robinson took her to nearby Bishopsgate Police Station, where she was formally charged and put into a cell by Sergeant James Byfield at about 8:45 P.M. Robinson then returned to his regular duties, and Eddowes was eventually released (see above).

Police Constable George Simmons

P.C. Simmons was walking his beat in Aldgate on 29 September 1888 when shortly after 8:30 P.M. he noticed P.C. Louis Robinson and a small crowd. The cause of the commotion was Catherine Eddowes, drunk and making noises like a fire engine. Robinson was having trouble getting Eddowes to her feet, but he managed to do so with the help of Simmons. Together the two policemen took Eddowes to Bishopsgate Police Station, where she was charged and put in a cell to sober up.

Police Constable Cartwright

P.C. Cartwright arrived in the small hours of the morning on 31 August in Buck's Row and was instructed by Inspector John Spratling to search the immediate neighborhood thoroughly. Spratling then went to the mortuary in Old Montague Street, where he discovered the extent of the injuries to the body of Mary Ann Nichols. Cartwright reported later to Spratling that he had discovered nothing to excite interest.

Police Constable Holland

City Police Constable Holland was on duty in the Minories on the morning of 30 September when he heard Kearley & Tonge watchman George Morris blowing his whistle. Holland arrived at once, and Morris directed him to Mitre Square, where P.C. Edward Watkins, who had discovered Eddowes's body, gave Holland further instructions.

P.C. James Harvey had also arrived; Holland was dispatched to 34 Jewry Street to fetch Dr. George Sequeira, whom Holland brought back at 1:45.

Police Constable Walter Stride (b. 1858)

The nephew of Jack the Ripper's third victim, Elizabeth Stride, P.C. Walter Stride served on the Metropolitan Police Force for twenty-five years. Walter Stride testified at the inquest on his aunt before Mr. Wynne Baxter and also identified the body in the mortuary.

Police Constable Richard Pearse

A member of the City Police, Constable Richard Pearse was living at No. 3 Mitre Square, next to the warehouse at which

George Morris was employed. The unsuspecting Pearse lay sleeping only feet away from where Catherine Eddowes was murdered. If he had been awake, he had merely to look out his bedroom window to see the Ripper. Pearse later stated that he saw and heard nothing until a policeman woke him up by knocking on his door.

Police Constable George Moulson (1862–1905)

A member of the Metropolitan Police, George Moulson patrolled the Whitechapel and Spitalfields areas during the Ripper murders.

Moulson was called to the river Thames on 31 December 1888 by waterman Henry Winslade, who had pulled out the body of Montague J. Druitt (s.v. ''Druitt'' in Chapter 3).

5. CORONERS AND DOCTORS

There were three coroners involved in the Jack the Ripper case, and a number of doctors. In this chapter, the coroners will be discussed first, then the doctors.

Several prominent doctors of 1888—such as Sir William Gull, the royal physician—are listed in the suspects category in Chapter 3.

For the most part, the doctors listed in this chapter either took part in postmortem examinations of one or more of the victims, or else were called to the site of the murder to pronounce death. Most of them also gave evidence at the inquest(s).

I have been fortunate to read reports by several of the doctors in reference to the injuries sustained by the victims, which are included either in part or in full under the name of the doctor who made them.

CORONERS

Wynne Edwin Baxter (1844–1920)

The coroner who was in charge of inquests on three of the Jack the Ripper victims (Mary Ann Nichols, Annie Chapman, and Elizabeth Stride), Baxter was a dynamic man who was also the mayor of Lewes, where he was born, and a published author.

Baxter opened the inquest on Mary Ann Nichols at the Whitechapel Working Lads' Institute on Saturday, 1 September 1888. It was reconvened on 3, 17, and 23 September.

Inspector John Spratling testified that he was called to Buck's Row at 4:30 A.M., 31 August, and afterward went to the mortuary where he discovered more extensive damage to the body after it had been examined at the scene by Dr. Llewelyn.

Others who gave evidence included William Nichols (husband of the deceased), Charles Cross and John Paul (who were on their way to work and came across the body), and Emily Holland (who may have been the last person, other than the killer, to see Nichols alive). There were a number of other witnesses as well.

After the second sitting of the Nichols inquest, Annie Chapman was murdered, and Baxter conducted her inquest also at the Working Lads' Institute, beginning on 10 September.

In the previous inquest, Baxter had been critical of the police, although it was Dr. R. Ralph Llewelyn who had examined the body in Buck's Row and failed to notice the full extent of the injuries. Baxter refused to let James Hatfield be badgered—it was Hatfield who stripped and washed the body.

In the Chapman inquest, which reconvened on 12, 13, 14, 19, and 26 September, Amelia Palmer gave evidence of her formal identification of the body, while Dr. George Bagster Phillips, H Division police surgeon, gave a detailed description of the injuries. Baxter decided to clear the court for the Phillips evidence, as it was graphic in nature and the Working Lads' Institute was hot and crowded. Several spectators had already passed out.

Phillips considered the mutilations to have been skilled, almost surgical, commenting that it would have taken an expert no less than fifteen minutes to perform.

In summing up on 26 September, Baxter exploded a bombshell when he said, "Both Nichols and Chapman had been murdered for some object, to secure some pathological specimen from the abdomen." These words were given wide publicity in the press, along with the story that a wealthy American had been offering large sums of money for certain organs in connection with a medical journal he was writing.

The *British Medical Journal* published a report on 6 October implying that this theory was erroneous, and Baxter made no further reference to it at the Stride inquiry. Inspector Frederick Abberline, however, believed it had some merit.

Baxter presided at one more Ripper inquest, that of Elizabeth Stride, which was conducted in the larger and more spacious Cable Street Vestry Hall. The inquest was held on 1, 2, 3, 5, and 23 October. Once again Dr. Phillips was the featured witness, although one cannot fail to question the omissions of such important witnesses as Matthew Packer and Israel Schwartz, especially when a scatterbrain like Mary Malcolm was permitted to give her worthless testimony.

Baxter was a flamboyant speaker and dresser who in retrospect seems to have conducted his inquests in a most respectable, efficient, and thorough manner. Baxter was also, by the way, a prominent Freemason in South Sussex Lodge.

There has been a great deal of argument that Baxter should have been in charge of the Mary Kelly inquest, as Miller's Court came under his jurisdiction, but the body was removed to a mortuary that was in Roderick MacDonald's territory. It is a great pity that Baxter was not allowed to conduct the Kelly inquest.

Dr. Roderick MacDonald (1841–1894)

A former doctor practicing in the East End and also a former police surgeon, Dr. Roderick MacDonald was in charge of the Mary Kelly inquest. It has been suggested that MacDonald was improperly called to sit on this inquest, as Kelly had been murdered in an area that came under the jurisdiction of Wynne E. Baxter. MacDonald, however, conducted the inquiry because the body had been taken to Shoreditch Mortuary, which lay in his territory.

Baxter had won an election against MacDonald the previous year (1887) for coroner of East London; MacDonald accused Baxter of tampering and other improprieties, which seems to have been just sour grapes on the part of the radical MacDonald.

The inquest on Mary Kelly took place on 12 November 1888, and, amazingly, was concluded after just a few hours. MacDonald, who seems to have had an exaggerated opinion of his own importance, instructed the jury to return a verdict quickly, adding, ''There is other evidence which I do not propose to call.''

While Wynne Baxter was thorough in his inquiries, MacDonald was quite inefficient in his only Ripper-related inquest. Mary Kelly was the last Ripper victim (which, of course, could not have been known at the time), and she was also the most horribly mutilated of the five victims. Trying to wind up an inquiry into her death in a few hours seems unbelievable, as there was much evidence omitted, not the least of which would have been the testimony of George Hutchinson. When we see that MacDonald allowed Caroline Maxwell to testify (someone who was patently confused as to dates—the medical evidence clearly refuted her testimony), one wonders what stupidity permitted this, as well as the omission of Hutchinson and others.

There have been suggestions of a cover-up here—that Mac-Donald was taking orders from a higher authority—but it would seem that is a bit farfetched. Rather, one would think Mac-Donald simply mishandled the case, and question the validity of his presiding over it. He showed little patience when dealing with the jurors, who were justifiably confused, and did not see fit to affix his signature to the certificate of findings signed by the jury.

Samuel Frederick Langham

Because Mitre Square lay in the square mile of the City of London, Coroner Samuel Langham presided over the Catherine Eddowes inquest. The inquest was held at the Golden Lane Mortuary, were Eddowes's body had been taken, on 4 and 11 October 1888.

On the opening day, Thursday, 4 October, Police Constable Edward Watkins was featured. Watkins, who had discovered the body, testified that Eddowes had been "ripped up like a pig in the market, her entrails flung in a heap about her neck."

A number of other witnesses testified that they knew the victim (such as Eddowes's daughter, and her common-law husband, John Kelly), while some merely told of what they had seen or heard on the night of the murder.

Dr. Frederick Gordon Brown, who was at the scene and later performed the postmortem, gave detailed evidence (for his complete report, s.v. "Brown" page 103).

Langham seems to have conducted the proceedings in a sober and competent manner, neither dragging it out unnecessarily nor speeding it through. It looks like all the relevant information and evidence was presented and no extraneous nonsense included.

DOCTORS

Dr. George Bagster Phillips (1834–1897)

Senior surgeon of H Division Police, Phillips was called to the murder sites of Annie Chapman, Elizabeth Stride, and Mary Kelly, and performed postmortem examinations on these three as well as on Catherine Eddowes.

In the Chapman case, Phillips was sent for and arrived about 6:30 A.M. at the backyard of 29 Hanbury Street. After pronouncing her dead, Phillips noted the contents of Chapman's pockets and other items lying nearby. He performed the postmortem at 2:00 the same afternoon, frustrated that Chapman's body had been stripped and washed before he arrived.

When Phillips arrived at 2:00 A.M. on 30 September in Dutfield's Yard in Berner Street, Dr. William Blackwell was already there. Along with Dr. Thomas Bond, Phillips was in attendance in Miller's Court, examining the remains of Mary Kelly on 9 November.

Dr. Phillips was an important witness featured in four of the five inquests on Ripper victims. His reports on the victims are herewith reproduced:

Report on Annie Chapman

The left arm was placed across the left breast. The legs were drawn up, the feet resting on the ground and the knees turned outwards. The face was swollen and turned on the right side. The tongue protruded between the front teeth, but not beyond the lips. The tongue was evidently much swollen.

The front teeth were perfect as far as the first molar, top and bottom and very fine teeth they were. The body was terribly mutilated.

The stiffness of the limbs was not marked but was evidently commencing. The throat was dissevered deeply, the incisions through the skin were jagged and reached right round the neck.

The abdomen had been entirely laid open, the intestines, severed from the mesenteric attachments, had been lifted out of the body and placed on the shoulder of the corpse; whilst from the pelvis, the uterus and its appendages with the upper portion of the vagina and the posterior two-thirds of the bladder, had been entirely removed.

No trace of these organs could be found, and the incisions were cleanly cut, avoiding the rectum and dividing the vagina low enough to avoid injury to the cervix uteri.

In this case, Phillips stated that he thought that he, himself a skilled surgeon, could not have executed all the injuries in less than fifteen minutes.

Phillips testified that he thought the knife used must have been six or eight inches long, probably longer, and that the killer had some skill or knowledge.

Report on Elizabeth Stride

The body was lying on the near side, with the face turned toward the wall, the head up the yard and the feet toward the street. The left arm was extended and there was a packet of cachous in the left hand.

The right arm was over the belly, the back of the hand and wrist had on it clotted blood. The legs were drawn up with the feet close to the wall. The body and face were warm and the hand cold. The legs were quite warm.

Deceased had a silk handkerchief round her neck, and it appeared to be slightly torn. I have since ascertained it was cut. This corresponded with the right angle of the jaw. The throat was deeply gashed and there was an abrasion of the skin about one and a half inches in diameter, apparently stained with blood, under her right arm.

At three o'clock p.m. on Monday at St. George's Mortuary, Dr. Blackwell and I made a post mortem examination. Rigor mortis was still thoroughly marked. There was mud on the left side of the face and it was matted in the head.

The Body was fairly nourished. Over both shoulders, especially the right, and under the collarbone and in front of the chest there was a blueish discoloration, which I have watched and have seen on two occasions since.

There was a clear-cut incision on the neck. It was six inches in length and commenced two and a half inches in a straight line below the angle of the jaw, one half inch in over an undivided muscle, and then becoming deeper, dividing the sheath. The cut was very clean and deviated a little downwards. The arteries and other vessels contained in the sheath were all cut through.

The cut through the tissues on the right side was more superficial, and tailed off to about two inches below the right angle of the jaw. The deep vessels on that side were uninjured. From this it was evident that the hemorrhage was caused through the partial severence of the left carotid artery.

Decomposition had commenced in the skin. Dark brown spots were on the anterior surface of the left chin. There was a deformity in the bones of the right leg, which was not straight, but bowed forwards. There was no recent external injury save to the neck.

The body being washed more thoroughly I could see some healing sores. The lobe of the left ear was torn as if from the removal or wearing through of an earring, but it was thoroughly healed. On removing the scalp there was no sign of extravasation of blood.

The heart was small, the left ventricle firmly contracted, and the right slightly so. There was no clot in the pulmonary artery, but the right ventricle was full of dark clot. The left was firmly contracted as to be absolutely empty.

The stomach was large and the mucous membrane only congested. It contained partly digested food, apparently consisting of cheese, potato, and farinaceous powder. All the teeth on the lower left jaw were absent.

Phillips gave evidence that in the Stride case the deceased had not eaten any grapes, and that death was, in layman's terms, caused by the cutting of the throat.

Report on Mary Kelly (inquest testimony)

The mutilated remains of a female were lying two-thirds over towards the edge of the bedstead nearest the door. She had only her chemise on, or some underlinen garment. I am sure that the body had been removed subsequent to the injury which caused her death from that side of the bedstead that was nearest the wooden partition, because of the large quantity of blood under the bedstead and the saturated condition of the sheet and the palliasse at the corner nearest the partition.

The blood was produced by the severence of the carotid

artery, which was the cause of death. The injury was inflicted while the deceased was lying at the right side of the bedstead. [For technical details of injuries and a much fuller report, s.v. "Bond" page 107.]

Dr. Frederick Gordon Brown (1843–1928)

Dr. Brown was the City of London police surgeon called in at the murder of Catherine Eddowes. Brown served in the police force until 1914, when he retired. He was also an officer in the Grand Lodge of England—a high-ranking Freemason. Brown testified at the Eddowes inquest.

Dr. Brown arrived at Mitre Square at two o'clock on the morning of 30 September. Dr. George Sequeira, who had been summoned from his Jewry Street surgery, was already at the scene.

Report on Catherine Eddowes

The body was on its back, the head turned to left shoulder. The arms by the side of the body as if they had fallen there. Both palms upwards, the fingers slightly bent. The left leg extended in a line with the body. The abdomen was exposed. Right leg bent at the thigh and knee. The throat cut across.

The intestines were drawn out to a large extent and placed over the right shoulder—they were smeared over with some feculent matter. A piece of about two feet was quite detached from the body and placed between the body and the left arm, apparently by design. The lobe and auricle of the right ear were cut obliquely through.

There was a quantity of clotted blood on the pavement on the left side of the neck round the shoulder and upper part of arm, and fluid blood-coloured serum which had flowed under the neck to the right shoulder, the pavement sloping in that direction.

Body was quite warm. No death stiffening had taken place. She must have been dead most likely within the half hour. We looked for superficial bruises and saw none. No blood on the skin of the abdomen or secretion of any kind on the thighs. No spurting of blood on the bricks or pavement around. No marks of blood below the middle of the body. Several buttons were found in the clotted blood after the body was removed. There was no blood on the front of the clothes. There were no traces of recent connexion.

When the body arrived at Golden Lane, some of the blood was dispersed through the removal of the body to the mortuary. The clothes were taken off carefully from the body. A piece of deceased's ear dropped from the clothing.

I made a post mortem examination at half past two on Sunday afternoon. Rigor mortis was well marked; body not quite cold. Green discoloration over the abdomen.

After washing the left hand carefully, a bruise the size of a sixpence, recent and red, was discovered on the back of the left hand between the thumb and first finger. A few small bruises on right shin of older date. The hands and arms were bronzed. No bruises on the scalp, the back of the body, or the elbows.

The face was very much mutilated. There was a cut about a quarter of an inch through the lower left eyelid, dividing the structures completely through. The upper eyelid on that side, there was a scratch through the skin on the left upper eyelid, near to the angle of the nose. The right eyelid was cut through to about half an inch.

There was a deep cut over the bridge of the nose, extending from the left border of the nasal bone down near the angle of the jaw on the right side of the cheek. This cut went into the bone and divided all the structures of the cheek except the mucous membrane of the mouth.

The tip of the nose was quite detached by an oblique cut from the bottom of the nasal bone to where the wings of the nose join on to the face. A cut from this divided the upper lip and extended through the substance of the gum over the right upper lateral incisor tooth.

About half an inch from the top of the nose was another oblique cut. There was a cut on the right angle of the mouth as if the cut of a point of a knife. The cut extended an inch and a half, parallel with the lower lip.

There was on each side of cheek a cut which peeled up the skin, forming a triangular flap about an inch and a half. On the left cheek there were two abrasions of the epithelium under the left ear.

The throat was cut across to the extent of about six or seven inches. A superficial cut commenced about an inch and a half below the lobe below, and about two and a half inches behind the left ear, and extended across the throat to about three inches below the lobe of the right ear.

The big muscle across the throat was divided through on the left side. The large vessels on the left side of the neck were severed. The larynx was severed below the vocal chord. All the deep structures were severed to the bone, the knife marking intervetebral cartilages. The sheath of the vessels on the right side was just opened.

The carotid artery had a fine hole opening, the internal jugular vein was opened an inch and a half—not divided. The blood vessels contained clot. All these injuries were performed by a sharp instrument like a knife, and pointed.

The cause of death was hemorrhage from the left common carotid artery. The death was immediate and the mutilations were inflicted after death.

We examined the abdomen. The front walls were laid open from the breast bone to the pubes. The cut commenced opposite the enciform cartilage. The incision went upwards, not penetrating the skin that was over the sternum. It then divided the enciform cartilage. The knife must have cut obliquely at the expense of that cartilage.

Behind this, the liver was stabbed as if by the point of a sharp instrument. Below this was another incision into the liver of about two and a half inches, and below this the left lobe of the liver was slit through by a vertical cut. Two cuts were shewn by a jagging of the skin on the left side.

The abdominal walls were divided in the middle line to within a quarter of an inch of the navel. The cut then took a horizontal course for two inches and a half towards the right side. It then divided round the navel on the left side, and made a parallel incision to the former horizontal incision, leaving the navel on a tongue of skin. Attached to the navel was two and a half inches of the lower part of the rectus muscle on the left side of the abdomen. The incision then took an oblique direction to the right and was shelving. The incision went down the right side of the vagina and rectum for half an inch behind the rectum.

There was a stab of about an inch on the left groin. This was done by a pointed instrument. Below this was a cut of three inches going through all tissues making a wound of the peritoneum about the same extent.

An inch below the crease of the thigh was a cut extending

from the anterior spine of the ilium obliquely down the inner side of the left thigh and separating the left labium, forming a flap of skin up to the groin. The left rectus muscle was not detached.

There was a flap of skin formed by the right thigh, attaching the right labium, and extending up to the spine of the ilium. The muscles on the right side inserted into the frontal ligaments were cut through.

The skin was retracted through the whole of the cut through the abdomen, but the vessels were not clotted. Nor had there been any appreciable bleeding from the vessels. I draw the conclusion that the act was made after death, and there would not have been much blood on the murderer. The cut was made by someone on the right side of the body, kneeling below the middle of the body.

I removed the content of the stomach and placed it in a jar for further examination. There seemed very little in it in the way of food or fluid, but from the cut end partly digested farinaceous food escaped.

The intestines had been detached to a large extent from the mesentery. About two feet of the colon was cut away. The signoid flexure was invaginated into the rectum very tightly.

Right kidney was pale, bloodless with slight congestion of the base of the pyramids.

There was a cut from the upper part of the slit on the under surface of the liver to the left side, and another cut at right angles to this, which were about an inch and a half deep and two and a half inches long. Liver itself was healthy.

The gall bladder contained bile. The pancreas was cut, but not through, on the left side of the spinal column. Three and a half inches of the lower border the spleen by half an inch was attached only to the peritoneum.

The peritoneal lining was cut through on the left side and the left kidney *carefully* taken out and removed. The left renal artery was cut through. *I would say that someone who knew the position of the kidney must have done it.*

The lining membrane over the uterus was cut through. The womb was cut through horizontally, leaving a stump of three quarters of an inch. The rest of the womb had been taken away with some of the ligaments. The vagina and cervix of the womb was uninjured.

The bladder was healthy and uninjured, and contained three or four ounces of water. There was a tongue-like cut through the anterior wall of the abdominal aorta. The other organs were healthy. There were no indications of connexion.

I believe the wound in the throat was first inflicted. I believe she must have been lying on the ground.

The wounds on the face and abdomen prove that they were inflicted by a sharp, pointed knife, and that in the abdomen by one six inches or longer.

I believe the perpetrator of the act must have had considerable knowledge of the position of the organs in the abdominal cavity and the way of removing them. It required a great deal of medical knowledge to have removed the kidney and to know where it was placed. The parts removed would be of no use for any professional purpose.

I think the perpetrator of this act had sufficient time, or he would not have nicked the lower eyelids. It would take at least five minutes.

I cannot assign any reason for the parts being taken away. I feel sure that there was no struggle, and believe it was the act of one person.

The throat had been so instantly severed that no noise could have been emitted. I should not expect much blood to have been found on the person who had inflicted these wounds. The wounds could not have been self-inflicted.

My attention was called to the apron, particularly the corner of the apron with a string attached. The blood spots were of recent origin. I have seen the portion of an apron produced by Dr. Phillips and stated to have been found in Goulston Street. It is impossible to say that it is human blood on the apron. I fitted the piece of apron, which had a new piece of material on it (which had evidently been sewn on to the piece I have), the seams of the borders of the two actually corresponding. Some blood and apparently faecal matter was found on the portion that was found in Goulston Street.

Dr. Thomas Bond (1841–1901)

A distinguished police surgeon (A Division) and former British army surgeon, Bond was called in on the final Jack the Ripper victim, Mary Kelly, In Miller's Court. Dr. Phillips was also in attendance. Along with Phillips, Bond conducted the post mortem examination on Kelly, and testified at her inquest. In a report Bond made to Sir Robert Anderson sometime later, he stated that he was of the opinion that the Ripper possessed no great surgical skill.

Although Bond did not see any of the victims other than Kelly, he nonetheless read physicians' notes on the various cases, which he mentions in the Anderson report. It is surprising that he thought the Ripper had no surgical skill when Bond knew that Kelly's missing heart had been extracted through her severed dia-phragm—not a job for a novice.

Bond's report to Anderson shed no new light and offered no unthought of hypotheses, although in the report Bond was the first doctor to delve into the more psychosexual motivations of the killer. Bond also believed that the Ripper, although "eccentric" or "not quite right in his mind" was probably a person whose day-to-day demeanor and appearance would give no one cause for undue suspicions or anxiety.

Bond concluded definitely that the five murders were commit-ted by the same hand.

Report on Mary Kelly

The body was lying naked in the middle of the bed, the shoulders flat but the axis of the body inclined to the left side of the bed. The head was turned on the left cheek. The left arm was close to the body with the forearm flexed at a right angle and lying across the abdomen.

The right arm was slightly abducted from the body and rested on the mattress. The elbow was bent, the forearm supine with the fingers clenched. The legs were wide apart, the left thigh at right angles to the trunk and the right forming an obtuse angle with the pubes.

The whole of the surface of the abdomen and thighs was removed and the abdominal cavity emptied of its viscera. The breasts were cut off, the arms mutilated by several jagged wounds and the face hacked beyond recognition of the fea-tures. The tissues of the neck were severed all round down to the bone.

The viscera were found in various parts viz: the uterus and kidneys with one breast under the head, the other breast by the right foot, the liver between the feet, the intestines by the right side and the spleen by the left side of the body. The flaps removed from the abdomen and thighs were on a table.

The bed clothing at the right corner was saturated with blood, and on the floor beneath was a pool of blood covering about two feet square. The wall by the right side of the bed and in a line with the neck was marked by blood which had struck it in a number of separate splashes.

The face was gashed in all directions, the nose, cheeks, eyebrows, and ears being partly removed. The lips were blanched and cut by several incisions running obliquely down to the chin. There were also numerous cuts extending irregularly across all the features.

The neck was cut through the skin and other tissues right down to the vertebrae, the fifth and sixth being deeply notched. The skin cuts in the front of the neck showed distinct ecchymosis. The air passage was cut at the lower part of the larynx through the cricoid cartilage.

Both breasts were more or less removed by circular incisions, the muscle down to the ribs being attached to the breasts. The intercostals between the fourth, fifth, and sixth ribs were cut through and the contents of the thorax visible through the openings.

The skin and tissues of the abdomen from the costal arch to the pubes were removed in three large flaps. The right thigh was denuded in front to the bone, the flap of skin, including the external organs of generation, and part of the right buttock. The left thigh was stripped of skin fascia, and muscles as far as the knee.

The left calf showed a long gash through skin and tissues to the deep muscles and reaching from the knee to five inches above the ankle. Both arms and forearms had extensive jagged wounds.

The right thumb showed a small superficial incision about one inch long, with extravasation of blood in the skin, and there were several abrasions on the back of the hand moreover showing the same condition.

On opening the thorax it was found that the right lung was minimally adherent by old firm adhesions. The lower part of the lung was broken and torn away. The left lung was intact. It was adherent at the apex and there were a few adhesions over the side. In the substances of the lung there were several nodules of consolidation.

The pericardium was open below and the heart absent. In the abdominal cavity there was some partly digested food of fish and potatoes, and similar food was found in the remains of the stomach attached to the intestines.

Dr. Rees Ralph Llewelyn (1849–1921)

A Welshman by birth, Dr. Llewelyn practiced in the East End of London, and it was from his surgery in Whitechapel Road that he was fetched by Police Constable John Thain to examine the remains of Mary Ann Nichols.

Arriving in Buck's Row at 4:00 A.M., 31 August 1888, Llewelyn noticed a small group already in attendance. After a very cursory examination, he pronounced Nichols dead, noting her cut throat.

By the time Inspector John Spratling arrived at 4:30 Llewelyn was gone, and Sergeant Kerby had removed the body to the Workhouse Infirmary mortuary in Old Montague Street. Spratling went to the mortuary to take a description of the body and make his report, and while there discovered that Nichols had been disemboweled. He sent a constable back to get Dr. Llewelyn once more, who arrived shortly to make a more thorough and complete examination.

Llewelyn also conducted the postmortem, and testified before Wynne E. Baxter at the inquest. Llewelyn believed the killer was left-handed, used an unusually long knife, and possessed a great degree of deftness and skill.

Report on Mary Ann Nichols

> Five of the teeth were missing, and there was a slight laceration of the tongue. There was a bruise running along the lower part of the jaw on the right side of the face. That might have been caused by a blow from a fist or pressure from a thumb.
>
> There was a circular bruise on the left side of the face, which also might have been inflicted by the pressure of the fingers.
>
> On the left side of the neck, about one inch below the jaw, there was an incision about four inches in length and ran from a point immediately below the ear. On the same side, but an inch below, and commencing about an inch in front of it, was a circular incision which terminated at a point about three inches below the right jaw. That incision completely severed all the tissues down to the vertebrae.
>
> The large vessels of the neck on both sides were severed. The incision was about eight inches in length. The cuts must

have been caused by a long-bladed knife, moderately sharp, and used with great violence. No blood was found on the breast, either of the body or clothes.

There were no injuries about the body until just about the lower part of the abdomen. Two or three inches from the left side was a wound running in a jagged manner. The wound was a very deep one, and the tissues were cut through. There were several incisions running across the abdomen. There were also three or four similar cuts running downwards, on the right side, all of which had been caused by a knife which had been used violently and downwards. The injuries were from left to right, and might have been done by a left-handed person. All the injuries had been caused by the same instrument.

Dr. George Sequeira (1859–1926)

A local practitioner in the Whitechapel-Spitalfields neighborhood, Dr. Sequeira was fetched from his surgery at 34 Jewry Street by Police Constable Holland on 30 September for the Catherine Eddowes murder.

Sequeira arrived at 1:45 A.M. at Mitre Square and pronounced Eddowes dead. He waited fifteen minutes until City Police surgeon Dr. Frederick Gordon Brown arrived, about 2:00 A.M.

Sequeira assisted Brown, Dr. Sedgwick Saunders, and Dr. G. B. Phillips at the Eddowes postmortem.

Sequeira also gave evidence at the inquest, and was quoted in a newspaper article as referring to the Ripper as ''no stranger to the knife.''

Dr. William Sedgwick Saunders

A doctor and officer of health for the city of London, Saunders observed and assisted at the Eddowes postmortem at Golden Lane Mortuary.

Saunders gave evidence on 4 October, at the inquest headed by Samuel Langham, testifying mostly as to the analysis of the stomach contents.

Saunders also gave an interview to the *Evening News,* following the examination of the kidney (by Drs. Openshaw and Sutton) received by George Lusk, in which he stated the liver was healthy. He also stated that the right kidney was healthy, which is a curious statement since Dr. Brown, and not Saunders, had tested it and found that it contained Bright's disease.

Dr. William Blackwell (1851–1900)

Sometimes referred to as Dr. Frederick Blackwell. Police Constable Edward Collins fetched Blackwell to Dutfield's Yard in Berner Street, where the doctor arrived at 1:14 A.M., 30 September 1888.

Blackwell testified that except for the extremities the body was quitę warm, further stating that Stride had been dead for less than twenty minutes. Along with Dr. Phillips, Blackwell took part in the postmortem examination.

Dr. Thomas Openshaw (1856–1929)

A curator of London Hospital's Anatomical Museum and anatomy lecturer and teacher at London Hospital, Openshaw examined the kidney that George Lusk received in the mail on 16 October 1888. Openshaw noted that the kidney was human and had been preserved in spirits of wine for about two to three weeks. It also contained a length of renal artery attached that exactly fit the piece left in Eddowes's body; therefore, it is most likely that Lusk received Eddowes's kidney from the Ripper.

Dr. Henry Sutton

Considered to be the foremost authority in England at the time of the Ripper murders on the kidney and its diseases. Henry Sutton checked out the kidney received by George Lusk at the request of Sir Henry Smith. A senior surgeon at London Hospital, Sutton stated postively that the kidney had been put in spirits of wine immediately after it was removed from the body, and was, therefore, no mere medical student hoax—as some had implied.

Dr. Thomas Barnardo (1845–1905)

Most famous for his homes for wayward and destitute lads, Dr. Thomas Barnardo visited the East End during the Jack the Ripper murders, trying in part to assist the children of prostitutes.

The significance of Barnardo is that he saw Elizabeth Stride in the kitchen of her lodging house in Flower and Dean Street shortly before she was killed. He subsequently identified her body in the mortuary.

Dr. William Holt (b. 1863)

The Jack the Ripper murders occurred while Holt was still a young intern at St. George's Hospital.

In an attempt to trap the killer, Holt frequented the East End, adopting certain disguises. Made up in blackface with white eyes, Holt frightened a woman the evening or early morning of 11 November, two days after the Kelly murder. The woman screamed, attracting a crowd which began beating Holt. Fortunately, the police arrived and took Holt away before he was seriously hurt. Holt's story and proof of identity apparently satisfied them, and he was released.

Dr. Benjamin Howard (1836–1900)

A distinguished surgeon and author in both England and the United States, Howard came to light in 1895 in an article in a Chicago newspaper.

The article stated that Howard had sat on a panel of doctors who supposedly put in an asylum, a renowed physician who was actually Jack the Ripper (implying Royal Court Physician Sir William Gull). Howard responded by denying the story and threatening to sue the newspaper.

6. MISCELLANEOUS

The following individuals are listed in this chapter for the simple reason that they do not meet any of the criteria or data for inclusion under any of the other chapter headings.

These people have a direct bearing on or played a significant part in the Whitechapel investigation. I apologize if I have left out any relevant individuals.

Robert James Lees (1849–1931)

Robert James Lees was a medium or clairvoyant who was supposed to have contacted Prince Albert from "the other side" after his death in 1868. After this, he was known as the Royal Medium; Queen Victoria had been much in love with her late husband and mourned his death until her own thirty-three years later. Having had some dreams, or visions, of the Whitechapel murders, Lees went to the police early in the investigation. For the most part, they took Lees for a crank or a hoaxer.

Lees allegedly saw the Ripper on a bus, then trailed him to a large house in London's fashionable West End. The police, who accompanied Lees, discovered the house was owned by a well-known surgeon who told them that he suffered occasional memory loss and had once had blood on his shirt that he could not account for. This story seems to be a fabrication, although Lees did not deny it when it was published in a newspaper some years after the killings. It has not been verified, although it has been stated that Lees received certain gifts as well as a government pension for his assistance to the police in their investigations.

George Lusk (1839–1919)

George Lusk was a small-business man residing in the East End of London. On the 10 September 1888, the opening day of the

Annie Chapman inquest, sixteen businessmen gathered together in the late afternoon at the Crown public house in Mile End Road. They formed the Whitechapel Vigilance Committee and elected George Lusk its president.

The committee offered assistance to the police and was praised by Sir Charles Warren. The committee made itself available to the public, offering to listen to any suggestions and pass them on to the authorities. The suggestion made most frequently was to offer a reward.

On 16 October, Lusk received a small cardboard box in the mail. It contained a letter and a human kidney, which was supposed to have come from Catherine Eddowes. The letter (see Chapter 8 for a full account) was addressed to Lusk, and in essence told him to be patient, and finished with the salutation "Catch me if you can Mishter Lusk."

In light of the fact that the kidney was almost certainly taken from Eddowes, it seems logical to conclude that the letter was genuinely from the Ripper, or at least someone who knew his identity.

Drs. Thomas Openshaw and Henry Sutton both examined the kidney, agreed that it was the "ginny" kidney of a forty-five-year-old afflicted with Bright's disease. Dr. Frederick G. Brown's report offers corroborating evidence. The kidney was preserved in spirits of wine shortly after its extraction. The doctors estimated that the kidney had been in the wine from two to three weeks. Eddowes had been killed seventeen days before it was examined. Also, the length of renal artery attached to the kidney received by Lusk exactly corresponded to the piece that remained in Eddowes's body. This then was no medical student's prank, as Lusk had at first supposed.

Reverend Samuel Barnett (1846–1904)

A well-known social reformer of his day, rector of St. Jude's and founder of Toynbee Hall, Whitechapel, Reverend Barnett was often quoted in newspapers which elicited his opinions during the Jack the Ripper murders.

Toynbee Hall was a place where anyone was welcome, and Barnett especially encouraged students to come there to help the poor by assisting in the necessary social work.

Barnett was particularly interested in getting better lighting for the Whitechapel area. His wife drafted a petition and collected four thousand signatures, which were sent to the queen, drawing her attention to the problems of vice and poverty in the area. It implored her to have all brothels closed down by putting into effect laws that were on the books but little used.

Barnett also wrote to the police, urging them to increase the number of patrolling constables in the area, and suggested that the wealthy should buy up the slum dwellings and turn them into inexpensive model housing.

L. S. Forbes Winslow (1843–1913)

Forbes Winslow was a qualified doctor and student of the law who was prominently featured in the Whitechapel investigation.

Winslow was convinced that he had learned the identity of Jack the Ripper, thanks to information communicated to him by a Mr. Callaghan, who thought the murderer was his lodger, G. Wentworth Bell Smith. Winslow put himself at the disposal of Scotland Yard, and told them that given enough men he could catch the Ripper. He suggested that all lunatic asylums be questioned regarding those inmates who had either escaped or been discharged.

Winslow believed the Ripper to be a man of respectable appearance who did not himself realize that he was the killer; rather, the murders occurred while he was in a state of shock or having some kind of fit.

Winslow was quoted on numerous occasions at the time of the killings, but lost some of his credibility through the years by changing or modifying his views. He was especially critical of the police, believing that they lacked imagination and would not catch so clever a criminal by conventional methods. In this he was absolutely correct.

A man knowledgeable in the realm of psychiatry, which in 1888 was still in its infancy, Winslow was perhaps ahead of his time with some of his suggestions. In his memoirs and in later recollections, Winslow always felt that it was because of him and the publicity he received that the murders eventually ceased. "If I did not arrest the murderous hand of Jack the Ripper, who did, and what part did they play in the transaction?" he later asked.

Samuel Montagu (1832–1911)

Montagu was the member of Parliament for the Whitechapel district at the time of the Jack the Ripper murders. A noted philanthropist who contributed to many charities—those of the East End in particular—Montagu met with George Lusk following the formation of the Whitechapel Vigilance Committee on 10 September.

The following day—11 September—Montagu offered a personal reward of £100 for information that would lead to the capture of Jack the Ripper. The lord mayor of London then offered £500 in the name of the Corporation of the City of London. A reward poster was ironically tacked up on a wall outside Miller's Court, where Mary Kelly was killed on 9 November.

Montagu also communicated and liaised with Henry Matthews and the Home Office at the time of the murders, offering his own ideas as well as passing on petitions and suggestions that had been made by individuals and the Vigilance Committee.

Henry Winslade (b. 1860)

Henry Winslade was a waterman who discovered the body of suspect Montague J. Druitt floating in the Thames. Winslade was in a boat on the river at 1:00 P.M. on the afternoon of 31 December 1888—a Monday—when he noticed the body. Winslade brought the body ashore in his boat, then located Police Constable George Moulson, who made a search of the body. It was then discovered that the deceased had several large stones among the possessions in his pocket.

Winslade testified at the inquest, which was held on Wednesday, 2 January 1889, in Chiswick, near where the body had been brought ashore. Winslade, who gave his address as 4 Shore Street, Paxton Road, had particularly noticed that the deceased was well dressed. The inquest returned a verdict of suicide while the balance of the mind was disturbed.

7. FREEMASONRY

Having attained the Sublime Degree of Master Mason, I believe myself to be more than competent to write something on the subject of Freemasonry, as it applies to this case. Freemasonry has not changed in the several hundred years since its inception, and is the same the world over (except, of course, that English and American Masons speak English, French Masons French, etc.).

Many authors of Jack the Ripper books, both factual and fictional, have speculated on the role allegedly played by Freemasons and Freemasonry in the Jack the Ripper murders. Some of these speculations are idiotic if entertaining, and I would venture that none of the authors I have read, and there have been many, is himself a Freemason. Otherwise, a great deal of twaddle would not have been printed.

Freemasonry is not and never has been a secret society; it has existed for hundreds of years and had scores of thousands of members worldwide. Its charitable aims and good works have been well known and highly publicized. As the character portrayed by Sir Anthony Quayle appropriately put it in the 1979 film *Murder by Decree,* "It is a benevolent society." And so it is.

One of Freemasonry's most perplexing problems is educating those outside its fraternity about just what Freemasonry is and what it is not. The secrets of Freemasonry involve certain rituals and business within the Lodge. Many groups, clubs, or organizations have "secret" passwords, signs, handshakes, and the like; Freemasonry is no different.

Masons wear certain ceremonial clothes and aprons, lapel pins, rings, etc., but openly march in parades, advertise the time and place of their meetings, and sponsor charities and school programs. This can hardly be called a "secret" society.

Many great men have been Freemasons, including kings, emperors, presidents, generals, admirals, business leaders, composers, entertainers, astronauts, scientists, sports figures, and

118

more. Men from all walks of life are Masons. That Catholics, Jews, or blacks are restricted or excluded from Freemasonry is one of the several misconceptions fostered by the ignorant.

Joining this fraternity is something we do for different reasons. Some may do it to be a better servant of humanity; some to make a deeper commitment to their own religious faith; others to help their brother members, widows, and orphans.

Masonry does not recruit its members; rather, the opposite is true. In my own case, I met a man who was a Mason, asked him about it, and was thus introduced. Although my late father had not been a Mason, my grandfather was and some of my other relatives as well, but I was either unaware of it or else they died when I was a young boy.

Qualifications to become a Mason are fairly simple and can be divided into two kinds: internal and external. One of the internal qualifications is that an applicant must come of his own free will and accord. The necessary corollary of this is that no Mason shall solicit other men to apply for membership.

Another internal qualification is that an applicant shall come uninfluenced by mercenary motives. He is not to expect business or professional advantages as a result of joining the fraternity.

The external qualifications can be divided under four headings:

Physical

An applicant must be a man, at least 21 years of age, and properly vouched for by at least two lodge members. To be eligible for the degrees he must be able to conform to the ceremonies required in the work and practice of Masonry. No person can undertake all the Masonic obligations unless he has reached years of discretion and is legally responsible for his acts. This rules out a young man under age; it also rules out a man in his dotage who has lost the powers by which a man recognizes and discharges his responsibilities.

Mental

The mental qualifications are not expressly defined, though a number of Grand Lodges demand that an applicant be able to read and write English. They are clearly implied, however, and are as binding as though explicitly expressed. Much is taught a Mason.

Much is demanded of him. It is impossible for him to understand such teachings, or to meet the demands, unless he possesses at least average intellectual ability.

Social

By this is meant all that has to do with citizenship and a man's life as a neighbor and member of his community. He must be under the tongue of good report—i.e., possess a sound reputation among those who know him best. He must be a good citizen and one who is obedient, as the Old Charges express it, "to the Civil Magistrates."

Moral and Spiritual

A Mason must be "a good man and true," a man of honor and honesty. So imperious are the fraternity's moral requirements that to speak of a Mason as not devoted to integrity and rectitude of character is a contradiction of terms.

It is required of an applicant that he believe in a Supreme Being. It is expected that all Masons practice tolerance and that no applicant be questioned as to the particular form or mode of his faith.

Freemasons will of course expel a member of the fraternity for certain violations of behavior; I do not mean something trivial like a parking ticket. Whatever the offense, no one is disemboweled or has his throat cut.

Many of the principals involved in the Whitechapel murders were Freemasons. Members of the Royal Family were Freemasons, as were most of the high-ranking government officials. Sir Charles Warren, Metropolitan Police commissioner, was a very prominent Mason.

The late Stephen Knight, in his well-done book *Jack the Ripper: The Final Solution,* a blend of fact and fiction, was the first to offer the suggestion of a Masonic conspiracy as the motive for the murders.

It seems that Joseph Sickert, son of the artist Walter Sickert, related to Knight a story of how his father allegedly had been involved with Sir William Gull, physician to the Royal Court, in the killings. The murders were supposedly contrived to silence the five prostitutes who attempted to blackmail the government.

Knight goes on to say that Prince Albert Victor, duke of Clarence and Avondale and grandson of Queen Victoria, had gone through a sham marriage ceremony and fathered an illegitimate daughter by Annie Crook, a Catholic shop assistant who was later lobotomized and institutionalized by Gull. Mary Kelly, supposed governess to the baby (and the final Ripper victim) told several other prostitutes, and together they attempted blackmail. Naturally they had to be silenced.

Knight suggests that the prime minister, Lord Salisbury, prompted if not actually ordered Gull to act, enlisting the help of Walter Sickert and coachman John Netley. *Murder by Decree,* the 1979 British-Canadian motion picture starring Christopher Plummer and James Mason, was based on this theory.

There are a number of facts woven into the story which make the tale the more plausible. Knight offers the factual writing on the wall in Goulston Street as evidence of a Masonic conspiracy. The writing, which was discovered by Police Constable Alfred Long at 2:55 A.M. on 30 of September, the early morning of the double murder of Elizabeth Stride and Catherine Eddowes, consisted of a chalked message on a brick wall at Nos. 108–119 Wentworth Model Dwellings, above a portion of Eddowes's bloodstained apron. The message read: ''The Juwes are the men that will not be blamed for nothing.'' Sir Charles Warren ordered the words to be erased from the wall, believing ''Juwes'' to be a misspelling of ''Jews,'' and fearing that the message would provoke anti-Semitic attacks and riots.

Knight purports that ''Juwes'' was a deliberate spelling, and referred to Jubela, Jubelo, and Jubelum, who slew Hiram Abiff of King Solomon's Temple. Now, Knight obviously was no Freemason; there is no reference anywhere in Masonry to ''Juwes'' being a term to refer collectively to Jubela, Jubelo, and Jubelum. Most of the other aspects of the story are plausible, and it is a fascinating tale. The prince's illegitimate child would have been more of a scandal at that time than a marriage to a Catholic, especially a marriage that was not valid. Walter Sickert did know ''Eddy,'' as the prince was called, and often used prostitutes as models, so he does form a link between the highest and lowest in the land.

Paul Begg, Martin Fido, and Keith Skinner are obviously no Masons either. In their excellent *Jack the Ripper A–Z* they state that Jubela, Jubelo, and Jubelum are revealed in the early stages of Freemasonry. This is a fallacy. These three names are mentioned only in the ceremony of the third or *final Masonic Degree,* when one becomes a Master Mason—and that is the highest level in Masonry. It has also been stated that Royal Arch Masonry is hidden from other degrees of Masonry, which is not true.

Of course, anyone in the general public, without being a Freemason, may know of the existence of Jubela, Jubelo, and Jubelum, and their significance to Masonic ritual. Anyone who has seen the 1979 film *Murder by Decree* will know about this, since it is the premise on which the film is based. And a number of books on Jack the Ripper, as well as on Masonry, discuss this point.

Those interested in or desiring to learn more about Freemasonry can go to their public libraries, most of which have a number of books on the subject.

8. POEMS AND LETTERS

The following poems and letters were written either at the time of the murders or shortly afterward. All had a direct bearing on the Whitechapel killings.

The police received as many as twelve hundred letters a week at the height of the Ripper scare. Some of them offered suggestions on how to catch the killer. At least one, from Edwin Brough of Scarborough, attracted the attention of Sir Charles Warren. Brough suggested the police use bloodhounds to track the killer, and offered the services of two of his champion hounds (Burgho and Barnaby).

Many of the letters were obvious hoaxes; however, only one person, Maria Coroner, was identified and arrested. On 21 October 1888, she was charged with causing a breach of the peace for sending letters to a Yorkshire police station signed "Jack the Ripper."

Two letters are thought by researchers to have actually come from the Ripper. They are the "Dear Boss" letter and the letter sent to George Lusk with the Eddowes kidney. Both are reproduced below.

The following poems appeared in publications or were sent to the police during the Ripper murders.

> I'm not a butcher nor a Yid;
> Nor yet a foreign skipper;
> I'm just your own lighthearted friend;
> Yours Truly, Jack the Ripper.

Here is another written at the time, which children of the East End still jump rope to:

> Jack the Ripper's dead,
> And lying in his bed.
> He cut his throat
> With Sunlight soap,
> Jack the Ripper's dead.

A poem that was published in a newspaper shortly after the incident between Sir Charles Warren and the dogs, ran thus:

> They brought him the bloodhounds, the best to be found;
> And the tecs and the dogs sought the murderer's ground;
> Then the bow-wows were loosed and with noses to earth;
> They trotted away mid the bystander's mirth.
> The bloodhounds grew gay with the fun of the chase,
> And they ran like two thoroughbreds running a race,
> They leapt o'er the wall and they swam o'er the stream,
> Their tongues hanging out and their eyeballs agleam.
> But Warren and Matthews kept up with them still,
> They followed through valley and over the hill,
> Then darkness arrived and afar in the haze.
> Hounds, Warren, and Matthews were lost to our gaze.

Following the execution of Frederick Bailey Deeming, a suspect in the Jack the Ripper killings, a certain poem ran:

> On the 23rd of May
> Frederick Deeming passed away
> On the scaffold did he say
> Ta-ra-ra-da-boom-di-ay
> Ta-ra-ra-da-boom-di-ay
> This is a happy day
> An East End holiday
> The Ripper's gone away.

Here is a bit of verse penned by Ripper suspect James Kenneth Stephen, which supposedly is a key to his sadistic nature:

> Oh mayest though suffer tortures without end
> May friends with glowing pincers rend thy brain
> And beetles batten on thy blackened face!

Here is the message found on the wall of the Wentworth Model Dwellings in Goulston Street by Police Constable Alfred Long following the double murder of Stride and Eddowes on 30 September 1888:

> The Juwes are the men that
> Will Not be blamed for nothing.

Several letters are noteworthy in that they may well have come from the Ripper himself. The first, which was received at the Central News Agency on 27 September 1888, ran as follows:

25 Sept. 1888

Dear Boss
I keep on hearing the police have caught me but they won't fix me just yet. I have laughed when they look so clever and talk about being on the right track. That joke about Leather Apron gave me real fits. I am down on whores and I shant quit ripping them till I do get buckled. Grand work the last job was. I gave the lady no time to squeal. How can they catch me now. I love my work and want to start again. You will soon hear of me with my funny little games. I saved some of the proper red stuff in a ginger beer bottle over the last job to write with but it went thick like glue and I can't use it. Red ink is fit enough I hope ha ha. The next job I do I shall clip the ladys ears off and send to the police officers just for jolly wouldn't you. Keep this letter back till I do a bit more work, then give it out straight. My knife's so nice and sharp I want to get to work right away if I get a chance. Good luck.

Yours truly
Jack the Ripper

Don't mind me giving the trade name wasn't good enough to post this before I got all the red ink off my hands curse it No luck yet. They say I'm a doctor now ha. ha.

This was followed by a postcard, also received at London's Central News Agency, on 1 October 1888, which ran:

I was not codding dear old Boss when I gave you the tip, you'll hear about saucy Jacky's work tomorrow double event this time number one squealed a bit couldn't finish straight off. had no time to get ears for police thanks for keeping my last letter back till I got to work again.

Jack the Ripper

Meanwhile, the police were getting as many as twelve hundred letters *per day*; here are three of the more interesting ones:

Dear Boss

You have not caught me yet, you with all your cunning, with all your Lees, with all your blue bottles. I have made two narrow squeaks this week, but still though disturbed I got clear before I could get to work.

I will give the foreigners a turn now, I think, for a change—Germans especially if I can. I was conversing with two or three of your men last night—their eyes of course were shut and thus they did not see my bag.

Ask any of your men who were on duty last night in Piccadilly (Circus End) if they saw a gentleman put two Dragoon Sergeants into a hansom. I was close by and heard him talk about shedding blood in Egypt. I will shed more in England.

I hope you read mark and learn all that you can; if you do so you may or may not catch.

Jack the Ripper

Beware I shall be at work on 1st and 2nd Inst., in Minories at twelve midnight, and I give the authorities a good chance, but there is never a policeman near when I am at work.

Yours,
Jack the Ripper

From Glasgow:

Think I'll quit using my nice sharp knife. Too good for whores. Have come here to buy a Scotch dirk. Ha Ha! That will tickle up their ovaries.

Jack the Ripper

On 16 October 1888, George Lusk, head of the Whitechapel Vigilance Committee, received a small brown parcel, containing a kidney, along with a letter, which was penned thus:

From Hell

Sir,

I send you half the Kidne I took from one woman prasarved it for you, tother piece I fried and ate it was very nise. I may send you the bloody knif that took it out if you only wate a whil longer.

> Signed
> Catch me when you can
> Mishter Lusk

A few days afterward, Lusk received another letter which ran:

> Say Boss, you seem rare firghtened. Guess I like to give you fits, but can't stop long enough to let you box of toys play copper games with me, but hope to see you when I don't hurry too much.
>
> Goodbye Boss

Thomas Openshaw, the distinguished doctor who examined the kidney Lusk received, also got a letter:

> Old boss you was rite it was the left kidny i was goin to hoperate again close to your ospitle just as i was goin to dror mi nife along of er bloomin throte them cusses of coppers spoilt the game but i guess i wil be on the job soon and will send you another bit of innerds.
>
> Jack the Ripper
> O have you seen the devle with his mikerscope and scalpul a-lookin at a kidney with a slide cocked up.

The newspapers and journals of the time also published numerous articles. Here is one that appeared in the *Police Chronicle* on 6 October 1888:

> The theory of these murders being attributed to foreign immigrants is now gaining acceptance. This theory is accompanied by another which touches the question of motive. In the view of some extremists in political causes all things are deemed lawful, however lawless they may be in other matters. It is said that a great cataclysm is expected to be accomplished in 1889. Proof of this can be found in a letter from an East End curate in which he foretold the rising of "a million men, all bent on avenging past neglect."

Here is the petititon drafted by Henrietta Barnett, and sent on to Queen Victoria:

> To Our Most Gracious Sovereign Lady Queen Victoria
> Madam:
> We, the women of East London feel horror at the dreadful sins that have been lately in our midst and grief because of the shame that has befallen the neighbourhood. By the facts that have come out in the inquests, we have learned much of the lives of those of our sisters who have lost a firm hold on goodness and who are living sad and degraded lives. We call on your servants in authority and bid them put the law which already exists in motion to close bad houses within whose walls such wickedness is done, and men and women ruined in body and soul.
> We are, Madam, your loyal and humble subjects.

On Saturday, 17 November 1888, a pardon was published in the *Illustrated Police News,* written on the tenth of that month and signed by Sir Charles Warren—after he had resigned.

> PARDON OFFERED
> MURDER PARDON. Whereas, on November 8th or 9th in Miller's Court, Dorset Street, Spitalfields, Mary Jane Kelly was murdered by some person or persons unknown, the Secretary of State will advise the grant of Her Majesty's gracious Pardon to any accomplice, not being a person who contrived or actually committed the Murder, who shall give such information as shall lead to the discovery and conviction of the person or persons who committed the Murder.
>
> >   Charles Warren
> >   Commissioner of
> >   Police of the
> >   Metropolis,
> >   Metropolitan
> >   Police Office
> >   4 Whitehall Place.

Finally, here is Dr. Thomas Stowell's letter to the *Times* of London, which was published the day after he died, 9 November 1970—the eighty-second anniversary of the Kelly murder:

Sir,

I have at no time associated HRH the late Duke of Clarence with the Whitechapel murderer or suggested that the murderer was of Royal Blood. It remains my opinion that he was a scion of a noble family. The particular given in the *Times* of 4 November of the activities of His Royal Highness in no way conflict with my views as to the identity of Jack the Ripper.

> Yours Faithfully,
> A Loyalist and a Royalist
> Dr. Tomas E. A. Stowell.

BIBLIOGRAPHY

Abrahamsen, David. *Murder and Madness.* London: Robson Books, 1992.

Acland, Theodore Dyke. *The Writings of William Withey Gull, Bart.* London: New Sydenham, 1896.

Adam, Hargrave Lee. *The Trial of George Chapman.* London: Hodge, 1930.

Alexander, Karl. *Time After Time.* London: Granada, 1980.

Alexander, Marc. *Royal Murder.* London: Muller, 1978.

Ambler, Eric. *The Ability to Kill.* London: Bodley Head, 1963.

Anderson, Sir Robert. *Criminals and Crime.* London: Nisbet, 1907.

————. *The Lighter Side of My Official Life.* London: Hodder and Stoughton, 1910.

Archer, Fred. *Ghost Detectives.* London: W. H. Allen, 1970.

Arlen, Michael. *Hell! Said the Duchess.* London: William Heinemann, 1934.

Atholl, Justin. *Who Was Jack the Ripper?* London: Reynolds News, 1946.

Barker, Richard. *The Fatal Caress.* New York: Duell, Sloan, and Pearce, 1947.

Barnard, Allan. *The Harlot Killer.* New York: Dodd Mead, 1953.

Barnett, Henrietta. *Canon Barnett.* London: John Murray, 1918.

Baron, Wendy. *Sickert.* London: Phaidon, 1973.

Baverstock, Keith. *Footsteps Through London's Past.* London: Shire, 1972.

Beattie, John. *The Yorkshire Ripper Story.* London: Quartet, 1981.

Beaumont, F. A. *The Fiend of East London.* London: Odhams, 1936.

Begg, Paul. *Jack the Ripper: The Uncensored Facts.* London: Robson Books, 1988.

Begg, Paul, Martin Fido, and Keith Skinner. *Jack the Ripper A-Z.* London: Headline, 1991.

Bell, Donald. *Jack the Ripper: The Final Solution.* London: Criminologist, 1974.

Bermant, Chaim. *Point of Arrival.* London: Eyre Methuen, 1975.

Binney, Cecil. *Crime and Abnormality.* Oxford: Oxford University Press, 1949.

Bloch, Robert. *Night of the Ripper.* New York: Tor, 1984.

Blundell, Nigel. *The World's Greatest Mysteries.* London: Octopus, 1980.

Boar, Roger, and Nigel Blundell. *The World's Most Infamous Murders.* London: Octopus, 1983.

Brewer, John F. *The Curse upon Mitre Square.* London: Simpkin-Marshall, 1888.

Brookes, John A. R. *Murder in Fact and Fiction.* London: Hurst and Blackett, 1925.

Browne, Douglas. *The Rise of Scotland Yard.* London: Harrap, 1956.

Butler, Arthur. *Was Jack the Ripper a Woman?* London: Sun, 1972.

Butler, Ivan. *Murderer's London.* London: Hale, 1973.

Camps, Francis E. *More About Jack the Ripper.* London: London Hospital Gazette, 1966.

Camps, Francis E., and Richard Barber. *The Investigation of Murder.* London: Michael Joseph, 1966.

Canning, John. *Unsolved Murders and Mysteries.* London: O'Mara Books, 1987.

Cargill, David, and Julian Holland. *Scenes of Murder: A London Guide.* London: Heinemann, 1964.

Cashman, John. *The Gentleman from Chicago.* New York: Harper and Row, 1973.

Chaplan, Patrice. *By Flower and Dean Street.* London: Duckworth, 1976.

Clark, Mark. *Ripper.* New York: Berkley, 1987.

Crowley, Aleister. *The Confessions of Aleister Crowley.* London: Jonathan Cape, 1969.

Cullen, Tom. *Autumn of Terror.* London: Bodley Head, 1965.

Daniel, Mark. *Jack the Ripper.* New York: Signet, 1988.

Davis, Derek. *Jack the Ripper: Handwriting Analysis.* London: Criminologist, 1974.

Deacon, Richard. *A History of the British Secret Service.* London: Muller, 1969.

Dearden, Harold. *Great Unsolved Crimes.* London: Hutchinson, 1935.

Dew, Walter. *I Caught Crippen.* London: Blackie, 1938.

The Diary of Jack the Ripper. London: Smith Gryphon, 1993.

Dilmot, George. *The Story of Scotland Yard.* London: Geoffrey Bles, 1930.

Douglas, Arthur. *Will the Real Jack the Ripper.* n.p., Countryside, 1979.

Douthwaite, Charles Louis. *Mass Murder.* London: Long, 1928.

Dozois, Gardner, and Susan Casper. *Ripper!* New York: Tor, 1988.

Emmons, Robert. *The Life of Walter Sickert.* London: Faber and Faber, 1941.

Fairclough, Melvyn. *The Ripper and the Royals.* London: Duckworth, 1992.

Farson, Daniel. *Jack the Ripper.* London: Michael Joseph, 1972.

Fido, Martin. *The Crimes, Detection, and Death of Jack the Ripper.* London: Weidenfeld and Nicolson, 1987.

Fishman, William. *The Streets of East London.* London: Duckworth, 1979.

Ford, Ford Madox. *Return to Yesterday.* London: Gollancz, 1931.

Fox, Richard. *The History of the Whitechapel Murders.* New York: Fox, 1888.

Franklin, Charles. *The World's Worst Murderers.* London: Odhams, 1965.

Friedland, Martin. *The Trials of Israel Lipski.* London: Macmillan, 1984.

Fuller, Jean Overton. *Sickert and the Ripper Crimes.* Oxford: Mandrake, 1990.

Gaute, Joseph, and Robin Odell. *The Murderers' Who's Who.* London: Harrap, 1979.

Goodman, Jonathan. *Bloody Versicles.* Newton Abbot: David and Charles, 1971.

Gordon, Richard. *Jack the Ripper.* New York: Atheneum, 1980.

———. *The Private Life of Jack the Ripper.* London: Heinemann, 1980.

Green, Jonathan. *The Directory of Infamy.* London: Mills and Boon, 1980.

Greenberg, Martin. *Red Jack.* New York: Daw Books, 1988.

Gribble, Leonard R. *The Man They Thought Was Jack the Ripper.* London: True Detective, 1977.

Griffiths, Arthur. *Mysteries of Police and Crime.* London: Cassell, 1898.

Hagen, Orlean. *Who Done It?* New York: Bowker, 1969.

Haines, Max. *Crime Flashback.* Toronto: Sun, 1981.

Halsted, Dennis. *Doctor in the Nineties.* London: Johnson, 1959.

Hanna, Edward B. *The Whitechapel Horrors.* New York: Carroll and Graf, 1992.

Harris, Melvin. *Jack the Ripper: The Bloody Truth.* London: Columbus Books, 1987.

Harrison, Michael. *Clarence.* London: W. H. Allen, 1972.

Harrison, Paul. *Jack the Ripper: The Mystery Solved.* n.p., St. Edmundsbury Press, 1991.

Hibbert, Christopher. *The Roots of Evil.* London: Weidenfeld and Nicolson, 1963.

Honeycombe, Gordon. *Murders of the Black Museum.* London: Hutchinson, 1982.

Howells, Martin and Keith Skinner. *The Ripper Legacy.* London: Sidgwick and Jackson, 1987.

Inglis, Norman. *Was Jack the Ripper Caught?* London: Titbits, 1962.

Jones, Elwyn, and John Lloyd. *The Ripper File.* London: Weidenfeld and Nicolson, 1975.

Jones, Richard Glyn. *The Mammoth Book of Murder.* London: Carroll and Graf, 1989.

Keating, P. J. *Fact and Fiction in the East End.* London: Routledge, 1973.

Kelly, Alexander. *Jack the Ripper: A Bibliography.* London: S.E.D., 1973.

Kingston, Charles. *The Bench and the Dock.* London: Stanley Paul, 1925.

Knight, Stephen. *Jack the Ripper: The Final Solution.* London: Harrap, 1976.

Larkins, E. K. *The Whitechapel Murders.* London, 1888.

Leeson, Benjamin. *Lost London.* London: Stanley Paul, 1934.

Lewis, Roy Harley. *Victorian Murders.* Newton Abbot: David and Charles, 1988.

Lilley, Marjorie. *Sickert: The Painter and His Circle.* London: Elek, 1971.

Logan, Guy. *Masters of Crime.* London: Stanley Paul, 1928.

Lowndes, Marie Belloc. *The Lodger.* London: Charles Scribners, 1913.

Lustgarten, Edgar. *The Illustrated Story of Crime.* London: Weidenfeld and Nicolson, 1976.

McCormick, Donald. *The Identity of Jack the Ripper.* London: Jarrolds, 1959.

McGowan, Bill. *Who Was Jack the Ripper?* London: Evening News, 1964.

MacLeod, C. M. *A Ripper Handwriting Analysis.* London: Criminologist, 1968.

MacNaghten, Sir Melville. *Days of My Years.* London: Arnold, 1914.

Masters, Brian. *Killing for Company.* London: Jonathan Cape, 1985.

Matters, Leonard. *The Mystery of Jack the Ripper.* London: Hutchinson, 1929.

Moreland, Nigel. *Jack the Ripper: A Final Word.* London: Criminologist, 1971.

Moylan, Sir John Fitzgerald. *Scotland Yard and the Metropolitan Police.* London: Putnam, 1934.

Nash, Jay R. *Compendium of World Crime.* London: Harrap, 1983.

Neil, Arthur F. *Forty Years of Manhunting.* London: Jarrolds, 1932.

Neil, Charles. *The World's Greatest Mysteries.* Neil, 1936.

Newton, H. Chance. *Crime and the Drama.* London: Stanley Paul, 1927.

Nicholson, Michael. *The Yorkshire Ripper.* London: W. H. Allen, 1979.

Oddie, S. Ingleby. *Inquest.* London, 1941.

Odell, Robin. *Jack the Ripper in Fact and Fiction.* London: Harrap, 1965.

O'Donnell, Elliott. *Great Thames Mysteries.* London: Selwyn and Blount, 1929.

Oliver, N. T. *The Whitechapel Mystery.* Chicago: Continental, 1891.

O'Neil, P. *Parting Shots.* New York: Life, 1970.

Parry, Michael. *Tales of Jack the Ripper.* London: Mayflower, 1975.

Pimlott, John. *Toynbee Hall.* London: Dent, 1935.

Pulling, Christopher. *Mr. Punch and the Police.* London: Butterworth's, 1964.

Quennell, Peter. *Mayhew's London Underworld.* London: Hutchinson, 1987.

Richardson, Joseph H. *From the City to Fleet Street.* London: Stanley Paul, 1927.

Robinson, Tom. *The Whitechapel Horrors.* Manchester: Daisy Bank. n.d.

Rosenwater, Irving. *Jack the Ripper: Sort of a Cricket Person?* London: Cricketer, 1973.

Rumbelow, Donald. *The Complete Jack the Ripper.* London: W. H. Allen, 1975.

Russell, Ray. *Unholy Trinity.* New York: Bantam, 1967.

Sharkey, Terence. *Jack the Ripper: One Hundred Years of Investigation.* London: Ward Lock, 1987.

Shew, Edward. *A Companion to Murder.* London: Cassell, 1960.

————. *Hand of the Ripper.* London: Sphere, 1971.

Smith, Sir Henry. *From Constable to Commissioner.* London: Chatto and Windus, 1910.

Smith, Terence Lore. *Yours Truly, from Hell.* New York: St. Martin's, 1987.

Sparrow, Gerald. *Crimes of Passion.* London: Barker, 1973.

Spicer, Robert C. *I Caught Jack the Ripper.* London: Daily Express, 1931.

Spiering, Frank. *Prince Jack.* New York: Doubleday, 1978.

Stephen, Sir Herbert. *J. K. Stephen's Poems.* London: Putnam, 1893.

Stewart, William. *Jack the Ripper: A New Theory.* London: Quality Press, 1939.

Stowell, Dr. Thomas. *Jack the Ripper: A Solution?* London: Criminologist, 1970.

Thomas, Donald. *The Ripper's Apprentice.* London: Macmillan, 1986.

Thomson, Sir Basil Home. *The Story of Scotland Yard.* London: Grayson and Grayson, 1935.

Underwood, Peter. *Jack the Ripper: One Hundred Years of Mystery.* London: Blandford Press, 1987.

Wagner, Gillian. *Barnardo*. London: Eyre and Spottiswoode, 1980.

Walbrook, H. M. *Murders and Murder Trials*. London: Constable, 1932.

Wensley, Frederick. *Forty Years of Scotland Yard*. Garden City, N.Y.: 1930.

West, Pamela. *Yours Truly, Jack the Ripper*. New York: Dell, 1987.

West, Paul. *The Women of Whitechapel and Jack the Ripper*. New York: Overlook Press, 1992.

Weverka, Robert. *Murder by Decree*. New York: Ballantine, 1979.

Whittington-Egan. *A Casebook on Jack the Ripper*. London: Wildy and Sons, 1975.

Williams, Guy R. *The Hidden World of Scotland Yard*. London: Hutchinson, 1972.

Williams, Watkin. *The Life of General Sir Charles Warren*. London: Blackwell, 1941.

Wilson, Colin. *Ritual in the Dark*. London: Gollancz, 1960.

Wilson, Colin, and Robin Odell. *Jack the Ripper: Summing Up and Verdict*. London: Bantam Press, 1986.

Wilson, Colin, and Patricia Pitman. *Encyclopedia of Murder*. London: Arthur London, 1961.

Winslow, Lyttleton Forbes. *Recollections of Forty Years*. London: Ouseley, 1910.

Woodhall, Edwin. *Crime and the Supernatural*. London: Long, 1935.

———. *Jack the Ripper*. London: Melifont, 1937.

Yallop, David. *Deliver Us from Evil*. London: MacDonald Futura, 1981.

INDEX